Stories of an Expatriate

Stories
of an
Expatriate

by
Otakar Machotka

Translated By
Jarmila Machotka

VANTAGE PRESS
New York / Washington / Atlanta
Los Angeles / Chicago

To my children,
Pavel, Jiřinka, and Hanička

Contents

An Almost Unnecessary Introduction

I do not know the accepted definition of the literary form "short story," but I do not think that Otakar Machotka's stories, which are in the reader's hands, quite pass the requirements of the classical short story of times past. They are rather sketches, *feuilletons*, newspaper articles, pictures in miniature of people, animals, and things. Mostly they are short studies that endeavor to penetrate from the surface of things into the depth of life. They are modern in that they reject old, pedantic literary forms; Machotka's stories are, rather, small essays, since, as I have written elsewhere, an essay is a form between science and art.

As you will see further, Machotka is like a composer who first selects his theme, then develops it either directly or with variations, and at the end finishes with a full-sounding coda, a general lesson that transcends the original theme. This, of course, is the typical form of the scientific method of induction, in which fantasy always works above the dry data of observation, a typical form for all experimenters and essayists, but one alien to the authors of classical short stories. It is not strange that Machotka bases his literary sketches on his knowledge of sociology, which is, as it were, illustrated and humanized by his stories. In his sociological studies I find the man everywhere, especially in his love toward animals and inanimate things. A grasshopper jumping on a concrete sidewalk, ladles in a bombed-out house, thermometers functioning even when no one sees them, give our author a pretext to show his love for weak and erring man, a love that for Machotka is a Christian redemption from his daily statistical and analytical sociological work.

The book that you have in hand, dear reader, is not only the work of a sociologist but also of an exile. The expatriation is not some outward sign taken out of the contents of the stories; it permeates all the works. We follow it between the lines; it shows itself in his love of the Czech language, the Czech book, in a patriotism that is not a decorative sticker but the essence of the author's personality; it shows itself in a patriotism that permits so many people walking around on crutches to walk erect and lively and see! Moreover, as a sociologist, Machotka proved with his book that exile itself is like a seismograph that registers many movements of the world and of life that would otherwise go undetected. It is a seismograph so fine that I am almost afraid to send this little book into the hands of those who have already ceased to be exiles.

Petr Den

Stories of an Expatriate

Ladles in the Wind

One bright day during the war, when the Allies were escalating their air offensive against Germany, American bombers flew mistakenly over Prague and dropped several incendiary and explosive bombs. Although the pilots recognized their mistake in less than a minute (they thought, by the shape of the river, that they were above Dresden) and stopped the bombing, in those few minutes fourteen hundred people were killed in Prague; many houses were either burned down or destroyed.

I was, as usual, in the office. We did not think that the attack was that serious. But on my way home, down in Nusle, I saw the first bloodied faces and a fright overtook me. On reaching my home I realized how serious the attack had been and that my family had escaped a direct hit by a mere hair's breadth: A bomb had fallen in the next block, striking the new car barn, and the large roof, made of some tens of thousands of glass panes, was completely shattered. Not until then did I experience fright at the closeness of the danger—and a feeling of gratitude that we had been spared.

For a long time afterward, as we passed the burned or half–bombed-out houses, we talked about the people who had died in them. Some of them we had known, and others we knew about because of their community activities. Daily we learned new details, and, while we were slowly recovering from the first shock, we learned to live with the realities.

Curiously, while our eyes got used to the frightful sight

1

and while our feelings grew duller, I became more and more intrigued with an anomaly brought about by the attack: It was the sight of ladles hanging on their hooks above an invisible stove, which had been knocked to the ground with its kitchen and half of the house. Strangely, the ladles had not been thrown down either by the bomb or by the impact of the explosion. They remained neatly in their places on the third floor of the house. There was a whole row of them, long and short; large and small; blue, white, and possibly of other colors. Their owner, who had neatly washed and arranged them according to size and had hung them before the attack, had been buried for some time, but the ladles somehow continued their life without regard for the loss of their mistress, without regard for the disappearance of the kitchen they had served, or for the half of the house that lay in ruins.

At first it seemed simply interesting, such as when a surgeon opens a man with a knife and exposes organs inside a body, which, all through a man's life, have grown and worked in harmony. It seemed a flagrant violation of a generally recognized privacy, for the kitchen is the private kingdom of a housewife, one normally protected from the eyes of people who pass by the house. No one has the right to lay bare and publicly expose the order on one side of the kitchen, not even when the inside of that house has been laid bare by the accidental impact of a bomb. This private world was usually shown only to intimate friends and then only on rare occasions; visitors usually sat in the living room, and the mistress of the house got up alone from the dinner table. By chance everything in this kitchen was in order. I have to salute this housewife. And, since she was already buried, we can say that she left behind a good example. But what an unusual example! In this respect she is certainly one in a million.

The oftener I passed the bomb-halved house, the more the ladles intrigued me. They remained steadfastly in the same spot. I have no idea why. How is it possible that no one came to take them down from their hooks? I suppose it was because the stairway had also been destroyed, and nobody could reach them. Above all, because they were only ladles? And, then, people may have had a certain respect for the unknown housewife who had hung them in a nice order before Death came for her.

The ladles clung to their spot, high above the street, for weeks and months; they formed a life of their own, since they were no longer in the hands of the housewife who had used them daily in a functional and useful way. They frequently changed their appearance depending upon which side the sun shone on them and on which side they cast their shadow. They changed color according to whether it was cloudy or sunny, but mainly they nodded in the wind, sometimes more, sometimes less. That especially gave them life, so that they looked as if they led a colorful and interesting existence. Undisturbed, they survived their mistress for months in the same order as she had arranged them.

It is not strange that things survive us in the way we had left them in the hour of our death. But not for long. Books are taken by our closest relatives, as are kitchen utensils or ties. Money is divided according to the last will, and a new tenant moves into our house. And, even if ladles remain, the closest relatives of the deceased housewife divide them among themselves. And, because they are of little value, this happens relatively fast and without much discussion.

But my ladles in the wind remained exactly as the deceased had arranged them. They survived the bombing while hundreds of people in the surrounding houses were killed. They survived undisturbed just on the very edge of destruction. Death passed close by but did not touch them. How strangely death behaves! We humans, after all, have more claim to consideration than ladles.

3

Two Raccoons

A few days ago I drove on the highway, and, as usual, I saw a few little animals who had been run over. I see those little carcasses on the road almost daily, and although I am always very sorry for them, I have gotten used to seeing them. I have to brace myself against excessive pity, especially since there is nothing I can do in the matter. In truth no one can do anything.

This time, however, I had to take more notice than usual of two carcasses. They were two raccoons; their bodies lay close to each other. They had probably been killed by one car. The first little body lay close to the right side of the road; the second lay nearer to the center and a little farther back. It seems that they were crossing the road together and that one was killed by the right front wheel and the other by the left rear wheel, thus dying merely a fraction of a second later.

It is surely extraordinary that the second raccoon proceeded a little farther ahead, at the distance of the left wheel from the right. It is a tragic coincidence that both raccoons met their death almost simultaneously. But my initial pity soon gave way to other reflections. It remained, but it was supplemented by a certain contentment.

Evidently a pair—we would say—of "lovers or spouses," they were joined by a bond of companionship, not by law or accepted morals. They enjoyed each other's company as animals can, spontaneously, without having any concept of friendship, fidelity, solidarity, or duties—let alone marriage.

4

They were drawn to each other; physical proximity was a source of pleasure. They spent most of the daytime or nighttime together, looking for food, hiding from enemies, playing, traveling together, and, during the mating season, enjoying the pleasure of physical contact.

Similarly they crossed the road together, and this "togetherness" remained a tragic chance even in death. But wasn't that in fact good? Was it not better, since one of them had to die, that death came for the other one, too? It spared him a lot of sadness and perhaps even suffering. It spared him the feeling of loneliness, aimlessness, restlessness, even if not the real mourning which can be felt by humans and to a certain extent by primates.

Reckless automobiles speeding along the highway day and night, at a pace the little animals cannot cope with, can kill not only without regard but also with mercy. Of course, it is unintentional. It is pure chance that by exception they commit an act that has in it something comforting—comforting, if the killing is unavoidable. In thousands or tens of thousands of cases each year, an automobile kills only one animal and causes sorrow and loneliness to the other.

Probably few of the drivers on this road noticed this double death, and fewer its mercy. Certainly the men who work on the highways would not have paid attention and would simply have removed the two carcasses like all the others. Why did it occur solely to me that an unusual thing had happened on this road? Is it because I am fond of little animals? Or possibly because I like to ponder the fate of living creatures? Or was it merely by chance? Whatever the reason, it left a deep impression, which even months have not effaced. Merciful car! Merciful fate! A kindly chance for an unusual though social death among the hundred of thousands or millions of other dyings.

Maybe it is not worth it to ponder one case for so long. The automobiles keep driving, and keep killing, and will go on doing so in greater and greater numbers. The wheels of death on the highway turn fast, while from under them little creatures fall in an endless stream. It is part of our civilization. There is no reason to talk about individual cases. But in spite of that I would like to place a little posy on the grave of these raccoons. They died just as masses of others have. Their bodies have disintegrated according to Nature's law. But I would regret if nothing survived them—if nothing else, at least this tale. They deserve it because of their exceptional fate, their comradeship, their mutual bonds for which I cannot even find the right words. If they had been people, I would say because of the strength of their mutual love until death. But they were only little animals, mere dumb creatures.

A Keycase

I carry my two car keys in an old, worn keycase; it is just big enough to hold them. Despite its worn state, I do not want to buy a new one. I am fond of this case: somehow it is a source of comforting and stimulating thoughts of which I am often not fully aware. Whenever I take it in my hand, I feel something familiar and friendly; I could almost say that life seems a little easier to me. Maybe this appears somewhat peculiar and exaggerated, especially if I tell you that, when I got the case, it was already used. Today, years later, it is in an even worse state. As a matter of fact, any sensible man would throw it away and buy a new one.

But I shall not do it. I shall gladly keep it for several years more, certainly as long as possible. You probably will say: "Well, people are strange and this is just a small and unimportant foible." I shall certainly not be considered abnormal or dangerous because of that, but neither will I be taken for a man who is absolutely rational.

In spite of that, I think I can persuade you that everything is all right with me. Perhaps, I differ from other people in that I sometimes notice things that other people do not pay much attention to and remember some of them vividly. That is probably all that sets me somehow apart from others. I believe that you will understand and accept what I have to say if I tell you the short and insignificant history of this keycase.

First I have to tell you that I did not buy the keycase; it

was given to me. It was, of course, a very small and insignificant present. And, if I feel any gratitude to the donor, it should be as slight, as the gift was trivial.

I was given this case under unusual circumstances. At that time I was "new" in the United States, and it happened shortly after I had bought my first car. As is usual, I received two sets of keys with the car, each pair held together by a thin wire. I should have bought a small steel chain or a leather case, but, since I was unaware of the existence of such devices for car keys, I left my keys on the wire, which served, if not well, then quite adequately.

With my keys on the wire, I once went to a gas station to have some small repair made on my car. I waited inside, near the cash register, to pay my bill with two other men who were waiting there for the same purpose. As the station owner returned from my car and handed me my keys, one of the gentlemen noticed the wire that held the keys together. He probably gathered that I was a foreigner and did not know American ways. He smiled at me and told me that this was not the way to carry car keys; they should be on a chain or in a case. I probably looked a little surprised, but the smiling man took something out of his pocket and handed me a worn keycase. I must have looked even more surprised then, for I did not know how to use it. So the man, still smiling, took the keys out of my hand, opened the case and put the keys in. He handed them back with an almost joyful expression.

I accepted the keys with the hesitation of a man who does not quite understand what has happened to him. That man assured me that this would certainly be better. Then he paid his bill and left with a smile. I remained in the gas station alone. I wanted to analyze the whole situation, clarify and understand it, but I was confused. Soon, the repair on my car was done, and the owner of the shop had returned. I could not continue with my meditation. I paid and drove off. However, the keycase and what happened between me and that man remain with me to this day. They make me aware of a man's interest in his neighbor, of a concern for his concerns, and they remain a symbol of human goodness and kindness.

Let us consider that this man had never seen me before and could not have had any other interest in me than the regard of one individual for another. His gesture was an expression of a general kindness extending to all people. He was probably willing to help any other unknown man, anyone who might need his help. Maybe his all-embracing kindness did not extend very far, and he might be incapable of great sacrifice on behalf of others. I do not know, and I prefer not to think about it.

Besides, it is not even that important. To me, it was enough that he was willing to render a small service to anyone, that he was generally a kind man and that he probably had a need to express his kindness to others. In truth, a worn keycase is not really a present; it has no monetary value. But this small present had a human value, a value of understanding a fellow man, a value of willingness to offer him a helping hand and to ease his problem. Maybe it meant only that the man at least thought of other people, and noticed their problems or needs. Even that means a lot in American life which, in its workday haste, has little time for anyone else. I am aware, of course, that Americans normally spend part of their leisure time and energy in charitable works and show an interest in others. But while at work, few pay attention to their fellows. This man went beyond the norm: "At work do your work, after work do your good deeds." He was kinder than some people are, and with his gesture he touched me deeply.

And so I still drive with this visible and palpable piece of human kindness. It warms my pocket and it warms my heart. It is a tangible expression of American kindness that strikes me tenderly whenever I touch it or look at it. It is a small but significant part of the optimism I keep, despite the hard experiences of exile. It heightens considerably what I like about America. It pushes some bitter experiences into the background, and tips the scales of my relations with this country to the positive side. It is like a good word, which somebody might repeat to me several times a day, and it outweighs the factual, dry, and perhaps unkind words I must sometimes hear.

Believe me, this present of a keycase made clear what the Americans mean by the expression "good-will ambassador." Without knowing it, this man was an excellent good-will ambassador. And his little present is a kind of permanent ambassador to my exile's soul. No, it is not a senseless expense or useless advertising when a good-will ambassador is sent abroad. Such ambassadors have their value, provided they are sensitive and good people. Of course, there should probably be more of them. And they should not always work in foreign countries.

And now that I have told you what kind of keycase I have, you will understand why I take good care of it and do everything not to lose it. And it is not easy. I have a tendency to forget things and misplace them. I have even left my keycase in several places. But amazingly, it has always come back somehow. And whenever I look for it, I look not only for the keycase, but also for the piece of human kindness it represents, for a piece of my faith in people, even for a piece of my own life. It is very important to me not to lose this symbol of humanity and friendliness. Such a precious thing no one wants to lose.

Grasshopper on the Sidewalk

At first I did not fully realize that it was a grasshopper that jumped in front of me as I walked on the concrete sidewalk of the main street of a little town. Not until he jumped for the second time did I notice him. Immediately afterward he made a long third jump. Apparently it was not I alone who frightened him, because several people came close to him from both directions.

Perhaps no one had frightened him. He simply did not feel good on the hot concrete and tried to get onto a patch of grass. I felt a little concern and stopped to see what he would eventually succeed in doing. It was, of course, foolish to believe that he could achieve anything no matter how hard he tried. He jumped for the fourth, fifth, and sixth time, and continued jumping. His jumps seemed longer and longer—at least some of them did—and all of a sudden I felt some desperation in them. I thought to myself: How far can he jump? What can he achieve with all his tireless trying? Can he reach grass at all so as to continue his life, so short in any case? He cannot. Every jump would undoubtedly end the same way. This unending struggle! That desperate effort! That fight for life, for normal living conditions! It was pathetic and overwhelming. Here a creature fights desperately for life, with all his energy, while hundreds of people pass by, not even noticing. And then comes someone who does notice, but does nothing and lets the creature fight its futile fight unaided. I felt ashamed, like

11

someone not doing his duty, like a hardhearted man who feels he should help but finds other things more important. But it was not a real guilt, rather a tendency to find fault with myself. When I wanted to help the poor grasshopper, I realized that I couldn't. I wouldn't even catch him. He was frightened, and his jumps were frantically fast and unpredictable. And then, could I attempt to help him amidst all those people going in both directions and thinking only how to get to a store or to an office or somewhere else as soon as possible? It wasn't even physically possible. I would get in their way, stop them, and needlessly interfere with their normal walk. I wouldn't achieve anything, and, on top of it, I would appear odd. It would hurt me in my occupation, which requires a certain common sense and dignity.

So I was reasonable, as were so many other people. But I could not help turning around to look. I saw the grasshopper near a pair of girl's legs, which at that time did not interest me at all. The girl was disinterested and indifferent, just like the milling humanity around her. I looked most of all at the grasshopper to which I owed something somehow and which somehow I could not fulfill. I saw more jumps. They seemed to me more and more desperate. How long can such a grasshopper jump before exhausting his energy? When will the last jump come after which there will be nothing? When will he sit exhausted on the hostile concrete in anticipation of a certain death? Or, perhaps—which would probably be the best—he will end in the midst of jumping with a kind of heart attack?

I am not a natural scientist and have no idea what the answer to this question is. It is in any case not that important. It is certain that the grasshopper fought a hopeless fight for life in which he had not the slightest chance of success. It is certain that the fight had to finish soon, that exhaustion and lack of food must bring the end in a few hours. In my mind I looked for some other possible and more acceptable solution than death by exhaustion or heart attack. At that moment I noticed that nearby was the grate of a street sewer. That seemed like the most acceptable, although equally hopeless, solution. Perhaps, in his senseless and desperate jumping, the grasshopper would jump through the opening of the grate and drown quickly. It would certainly be better than the endless, exhausting and equally senseless jumping. This thought quieted me a little, but the feeling of helplessness and depression remained. It is dreadful to fight so earnestly and hopelessly for life and not even be aware of it! To the grasshopper's feeling of horror and fright, the tremendous effort, the inhospitability of artificially created conditions, in which there was no room for him, were sufficient.

I don't know why the incident of the grasshopper on the concrete so moved me and spoiled the rest of my day. Possibly it was a little selfish. I myself am a little like the grasshopper transplanted into a surrounding from which I cannot jump to where I belong. Even though, unlike the grasshopper, I can survive on the American concrete, I am always trying to reach my own surroundings. But, in reality, I believe that was not in my subconscious when I so keenly felt the inevitable fate of the grasshopper. It was above all a simple sympathy with a creature who desperately and obstinately fights a futile life struggle. It was disagreeable to think that so many people were close to the struggling creature and did not even known of its existence, let alone feel for it or help it.

Life in nature is, of course, hard and from a human standpoint quite merciless and indifferent. But in this case it was something else. We know that lions devour gazelles and snakes eat frogs. It is a part of the order of Nature, inevitable and valid. But concrete is a product of man. It is an artificial condition of life, from the standpoint of Nature nonsensical and outside its order. And it is not the only such condition created by man. How many people are like the grasshopper on concrete, struggling desperately for something without an inkling that their endeavor is hopeless and necessarily leads to the unavoidable end! How many writers, defending freedom and human rights, perished in concentration camps! How many were tortured to death by the Gestapo! How many democratic statesmen died equally horribly in Communist states! And for how many people an instant death, like a jump into the grate for the grasshopper, would really be the best solution! There must be more than a few of them. It is only fortunate that most people are unaware of what awaits them, just like the unfortunate grasshopper.

Pots and Pans as Historians

Not long ago in the attic I came across two little containers, whose existence I somehow would have preferred to ignore. They were shabby, nicked, old, and ugly. In spite of that, we put them back and we shall probably keep them the rest of our lives. They are part of our history, or rather, part of the history of our family. They served as cups for coffee or soup in a refugee camp after we had fled our homeland in 1948. At that time, I was in another camp and did not bring over the cups I had used there.

These strange vessels were made out of empty cans with handles soldered to them. Otherwise they are of plain tin plate, and now bear the marks of age and use. Finding them again after almost two decades was a surprise to me. Could it really be true that we used such vessels, that we were so poor that we considered it a great advantage to own them? That, besides this possession, not counting the clothes on our backs, we owned practically nothing else? It is almost incredible how times have changed! For a long time now we have been leading normal lives; we can buy good pots and pans readily, and obtain any other necessities of daily life easily. And we have enough, all that we need and possibly more than we had at home. Production in the United States and the whole civilized world goes up, and so do sales and purchases.

These two containers are not only memories of the difficult times we lived through, but also part of our family chronicle.

15

They represent a simple but persuasive part of it, a decisive proof that this was the way we lived, the depth to which we had fallen, that we were so powerless that we gratefully accepted even such a poor and primitive thing as mugs made of empty cans. They connect with memories of the refugee camp in Germany where we then lived, of the miserable and scanty food we ate, of the fits of depression to which we were subject, of the uncertain future that troubled us, and of the sorrow over possessions left behind. There were the fears of the horrors of the Communist regime, the sorrow of leaving behind the loved ones we might never see again, the tragedy of a nation that was no sooner freed from one hell than it was subjected to another. We think of the many faces we used to see in the camp: good and evil, devoted and selfish, brave and dejected, but mostly friendly faces united with the others by strong ties of refugee solidarity. We remember the political and personal quarrels, the escape stories, the boasting of those who are always masters of the situation; we also remember the silent ones, who never talked about themselves; we remember the plans and hopes for the future, the debates about immigration laws and many other things so important to all refugees.

And these and similar vessels are also a history of our nation. At home, something so awful had happened that tens of thousands of people were forced to leave their homeland and live abroad under conditions which these cups symbolize. These vessels are witnesses of a terrible national illness, of a terrible time in history, witnesses more eloquent than written documents. Such containers belong in a museum alongside other testimonies of our country's past. More important than our personal and family story, they recount the history of a whole nation.

Such thoughts go through my mind because these two small containers, preserved in the attic, are so different from the pots and pans we use now and also, of course, from those we had used before leaving home. Yet there exist so many artifacts in the household we have had for decades that are also testimonials of our past, but that escape notice.

People (but not refugees) have pots and pans they received as wedding presents. Those are probably remembered the best. And we know very well when we got them. They are like a precisely dated historical document, an important document of the family history, better preserved than some of the torn and incomplete papers that historians have to deal with. Then comes the small tea service we bought for our children. Even that is an important landmark in the history of our family. But it is not so precisely dated; we know only approximately when we gave it to the children for Christmas.

Well, the rest of the utensils bought during our marriage were bought piece by piece, as needed, and are therefore dated only with uncertainty. But they also have their historical value. Many memories are associated with individual pieces. Maybe a certain piece was bought while our aunt was visiting us; another, more expensive one, was bought after much discussion between husband and wife; others were bought after a catastrophe in the kitchen during which several pieces were broken, and finally, still others were bought before the visit of a larger number of guests. Certainly other occasions gave us a reason to buy other pieces. And all those dishes, bought at various times, remind us of certain family situations and events; they are part of the family chronicle.

In reality we could piece together parts of the family history if we took one item after another in our hands and remembered the family circumstances when we got it, either by purchase or gift, who was visiting our family at the time, to whom we showed it with pride, how we used it for the first time, what member of the family was still alive, who was not yet born, where we lived then, what our financial situation was, and many other details. If it is a vase or candy box, our memories are richer. We know what flowers we used to put in it (on our birthday, on Mother's Day or Father's Day, before dinner guests, after an outing, and so on). A candy box reminds us of the donor or the occasion on which we got it or bought it. Of course, I am uncertain whether dishes include vases and candy boxes. Maybe not.

But let us take the lowliest of equipment, pots and pans, as we see them in the kitchens of old castles. Often I have admired such pieces, carefully polished (especially their copper bottoms) and hung on a row of hooks above the fireplace. This is not only a family chronicle, but part of the cultural chronicle of the times. Unfortunately none of those who made the pots and pans, bought or used them, is alive to tell us something about them. Just the contrary, the cultural historian has to guess from which period each piece dates. In spite of that, such castle pots and pans are part of a nation's cultural history or at least of its nobility. This is more true of china found in castles or the homes of rich bourgeois families. Some sets are two hundred or more years old. And to this are added many memories shared by generations. Here, of course, cultural history has a richer mine and obtains more information than from our kitchen utensils.

I have dealt mostly with kitchen utensils, because I was so strongly affected by the two little vessels from refugee camp. Yet how many other objects we have in our household which have family-historical value: books we have received at Christmas or for our birthday; pieces of furniture we bought after a promotion in the office; a doily sent to us by a good friend or acquaintance; a picture we bought at an exhibit; memorabilia we brought from a trip abroad; a fountain pen or a watch we received for a birthday; a television set bought after our wife's illness; and many other objects! If we thought about them and all they remind us of, we would have a pretty complete family chronicle. But we do not do it. We use these objects, we enjoy them, we keep them in order, dust them, but we completely overlook their intrinsic value. And I think it is a pity. How much joy we would derive from this detective-historical work and how much its result would mean to our children! Of course, life goes before history. We have our daily worries, we lack time, there are troubles with children and in our employment, and all this overshadows the historical value not only of the utensils, but also of the objects that are part of our daily life.

Hotel Room

How many little stories there are in each hotel room! How many people have succeeded each other there, how many have reacted to its four walls, to the little writing desk, to the view from the window or most likely to the ceiling as they stared at it before falling asleep! How many ideas went through their minds! How many troubles, plans, joys, fears, and other feelings, accompanied by images from the past or of a future to be feared or desired, were seen in this room by its visitors awaiting slumber! These pre-sleep images could make more than sufficient material for a long and perhaps interesting motion picture.

A different film could be made from letters that were written in this room. Perhaps most of them were brief, to the point, possibly only of a business nature. Yet there were certainly also letters to mothers, friends, newspapers and lovers. There must have been warm, friendly letters extending an invitation or expressing thanks for a beautiful evening. There were certainly letters of farewell, perhaps even letters before embarking on a trip to a faraway country. There were probably also desperate letters asking for financial help or a muted cry before departure from this world. They, too, would make an interesting film or a meaningful history of contemporary or recent life. But, for the historian, just as for anyone else, they are forever irretrievably lost. And it is a pity! I am certain that students of history or sociology could use these notes, thoughts, and letters of visitors as documents that would surpass in their immediacy, and perhaps even depth, much that the social sciences have brought out about life of the present or recent past. Unfortunately I have never heard of anyone interested in these sources, possibly because they are not and never will be really available.

And yet in the hotel room there were sometimes not only the registered guests but also their visitors, sometimes of the same sex, but very likely also visitors of the opposite sex. A series of conversations having taken place between the four walls of the hotel room would probably yield a colorful, interesting and probably dramatic picture of contemporary life. But not even that is preserved anywhere, nor will it be available either to authors or to scientists. The ideas, concerns, plans, and conversations taking place in a hotel room are irretrievably lost. And in spite of that, when you are surrounded by its four walls and see how the room is clean and tidy, how it awaits a new guest, you cannot but think what is hidden behind its affable cleanliness, which pretends that it welcomes you and has been waiting just for you. Its blank face seems to await the little events that will give form: the choice of book you will put on the night table, what sort of underwear you will put in the drawers, what you will throw on the chair, whom you will call on the telephone and to whom you will write. This, too, will fall into oblivion and will join the great number of events that have previously taken place in the room and that have left not the slightest trace.

This unceasing and always repeated erasure of possibly interesting happenings does not take place without human effort. People are even paid to do it as thoroughly as possible. Chambermaids wipe out each trace of a departed guest so that a new thread of events, entirely different from the previous one, can start. The history of a hotel room is full of artificially created pauses, which separate individual guests from one another. That's how it has to be. It is the condition of a successful beginning of each new chapter in the history of the room, the hundredth or perhaps thousandth one.

Yet I once succeeded in getting ahead of the artificial pause and so intercepted something from the immediately preceding history of the room I inhabited. Of course, it happens to many people that they are let into a room not yet completely tidied. But I also received a little explanation so as to understand the meaning of what I saw. In reality I saw very little, but it was interesting.

I have to tell you first that, as an exile, I have friends in many occupations, although at home they had made a living in quite a different way. One of them managed to work himself up into an influential position in a first-class hotel in New York so that he could occasionally let his friends rent a room at a reduced price.

During one of my visits to New York, my friend took me into a room that was not yet quite tidy. The guest had left a moment before, after having used it for only half a day, but he had left a slight trace behind. It was a tray with two glasses, two half-empty bottles of Seven-Up, and a small bowl of peanuts. Some nuts were scattered over the tray, and in one glass there was a small amount of soft drink. My friend added that the guest probably was not a generous host. At that moment I noticed that on the tray there was also a crumpled napkin with a little lipstick on it. Immediately afterwards came the chambermaid to take the tray away. She made the "pause" between two histories of the hotel room.

I learned nothing more about the previous guests. But I kept thinking of them. They were probably not married. She may have been a prostitute. Possibly she was a secretary with her employer. Perhaps it was a chance acquaintance from the train or from the movies. Or perhaps something else still. But one thing was certain. That man wanted to make an impression of someone of a higher class. He went into a good hotel. Maybe even paid the lady well. But he was disproportionately careful about his hospitality. He did not offer a highball or cognac or even wine, just two small glasses of soft drink. And maybe he was not even ashamed. Perhaps he was a puritan—at least a puritan as far as alcohol was concerned. But that should not have prevented him from offering something to the lady; he did not have to drink himself. Yes, people are strange. And they are not always cavaliers. People like him try to keep up appearances. He went to a very good hotel for a purpose he wanted to hide from the eyes of the world. Therefore he kept appearances only before the lady. And then he made the excuse that he was a nondrinker or something similar. He made a bow to decorum but he failed. Such an excuse evidently could not satisfy the lady. Moreover, his frugality somehow contradicted the purpose that brought him to the hotel. A little bit of alcohol helps the partners to forget and to overcome a certain embarrassment. But the cautious man did not want to spend on that.

Now you see what I had in mind when I talked about the unknown history of hotel rooms. By chance, I had uncovered traces of a fresh history. But it is good that the couple does not know about it. They would resent someone writing about them or even putting it in print. The very idea that someone was interested in them, analyzed and criticized their behavior, would trouble them. Yes, I think it is very good that the histories of hotel rooms are not recorded. People have a right to privacy even in such a public institution as a hotel.

It is equally true that under other conditions people do not enjoy the accepted right to privacy. If an author, who later becomes famous, writes a letter to his mistress, it is something as private as the event in a hotel room. But it is likely that after his death the letter will be published in some literary study. As long as he lives, the author manages to defend his right to privacy, but after death he loses it. With the consent of the public the literary historians take it away from him. And nobody protests! How much more decent are the owners of the hotels! But if we look at it from the standpoint of literary history, how much richer would be research into the lives of famous men and women if events in hotel rooms were recorded and were available to writers, curious about the lives and works of literary personages!

A Little Heap of Dirt

A few years ago we bought a house, which we happily inhabit to this day. It is a large house with asbestos-shingle siding, which does not have to be painted every three years. This siding was put on just before we purchased it, while we were still our landlady's tenants, and it was not the only thing she left for us. In the garage there were many gardening tools; in the attic there were an old steamer trunk and an old school diploma (she was a hairdresser); in the cellar she left a very old romantic picture of a young lady with long, flowing hair, sitting in a boat. It was a print from the mid-nineteenth century. These and many other items remained in their places even after the old lady died. Yes, man's possessions remain much longer than he himself; they often live inconspicuously for years, sometimes even centuries or thousands of years. Greek statues or treasures from Egyptian tombs are just that; they, too, were parts of someone's life who passed away a long time ago and of whom nothing remains, not even a mummy in a museum.

But the old lady also left behind some things of a different nature. Death did not completely erase her existence even after a number of years. One of these residua was a little heap of dirt, which, from the beginning of our stay in the house, was at the right side of the driveway to the garage. We accepted it as something natural and never gave a thought as to how it got there and why it was there. We even thought that it was there for us, more precisely for our cats, who needed dirt for their box in the cellar. For a long time it did not occur to anybody to wonder why the little heap was there, where it had come from, and why someone had piled it there.

Not until recently did the explanation of something, that we did not even try to explain, occur to me, and it was solely because a strange thing happened. A portion of our lawn sank quite deeply into the ground, creating a wide sunken area. At first we were really surprised: there was no water under the ground or anything else—and all of a sudden such a deep depression in the lawn!

What to do? It had to be filled somehow. It was up to me and the first problem I faced was where to find the fill. In a town there is no superfluous, freely accessible dirt that anyone can take, which nobody cares about. But in our case there was an exception. We had that little heap of dirt, which I could readily use to fill the depression. Carefully, I took off the sod and carried one shovelful after another to fill the gaping hole. I used up all the dirt from the little heap, and to my surprise, just managed to level the depression. All in all it was some twenty-five shovelfuls of dirt. I replaced the sod with care, and the problem seemed solved. I knew that after a time the dirt would settle a little, and that I would have to add some more. But that would be for later.

The depression was gone, but the mystery remained. However, a sensible man does not contemplate such trivial mysteries. Therefore we dismissed the unexplained problem from our minds. Yet, one aspect of the matter was striking. How was it possible that the heap of dirt fit almost exactly into the depression? Except for what would have to be added later, the dirt and the hole matched. The missing amount we had probably taken for our cats. And then I recalled what our landlady had once told me: that she used to have a little dog whom she had loved very much and who had died. She reputedly had buried him in the backyard, probably in the same spot where the dirt had sunk in. The little dog was probably buried in a wooden box, the top of which had fallen through.

When the heartbroken old lady had ordered a grave to be dug for her little dog, the dirt had to be placed somewhere. Undoubtedly she had it transferred to the place next to the garage, which was inconspicuous and could not be seen because there was some underbrush. And now, years later, when the little dog, who had been part of the old lady's life, rotted away, the dirt was brought back to its old place. Unknowingly I had erased one of the many traces of her life previously reflected in the arrangement of things around and inside our house. Many of them, of course, will remain. They will remain even after our house again changes hands from ours to those of our unknown successor, and perhaps even from his to those of the next. We all leave traces about which no one may know were part of our lives. Our life will someday end, but the furrow tilled by it will be partly preserved. Perhaps it will be interrupted by someone, changed or, in places, even erased, but something of it will remain. Many, many years ago, someone invented a dot above the i. We do not know who it was, but this dot has been preserved for a thousand years, and millions of people continue to use it.

Other traces of our life, of course, will be erased or changed so as not to be recognizable. Few, however, will disappear as completely as the trace of our landlady, left behind in the little heap of dirt by the garage. The dirt that had been dug out years before had come back to its original place. The box in which the little dog was buried disintegrated; the little dog rotted away while our landlady also decays in the cemetery. Her great love for her poor little dog came to an end, and finally the last trace which this love left in the little heap of dirt came to an end, too. And I was the one who unknowingly erased this part of her former life.

A Hunting Hat

I had known Mr. Joseph Novotný for many years, although never intimately. He was a clerk in my department and used to come to me at least once a week to show me what work he had finished and to discuss what was to be done next. These discussions were not pleasant because Mr. Novotný was not exactly talented. It was difficult for him to grasp what I wanted and even more so to carry it out. I almost always found some flaws in his work, which he tried to explain agreeably, even if not satisfactorily.

For years Mr. Novotný was not promoted. Furthermore, he was in the lowest category of civil servants, and a promotion would have helped only very little anyway. Mr. Novotný could best be characterized as a little man who could expect to remain a little man all his life. In his category even talented people never got anywhere, let alone someone who lacked so much to give his supervisors satisfactory work. But the little he had was secure, and he could build his life on it in a very modest manner. And there are so many ways to build a life, to adjust to conditions in which we live, and to satisfy at least some of our wishes! Mr. Novotný found his own way. It was a small, almost trite, way of leading his life, but it was his, and it must have brought him contentment.

Indeed, it was not easy for him to find his own lifestyle and a certain degree of satisfaction in it. Mr. Novotný was a complete scatterbrain who had to apologize for something all the time. In whatever he did, he made mistakes; he had no ideas, nor was he efficient. Even in his marriage he must have had a subordinate position (at least I thought so), and all this made him a man with an inferiority complex. His whole conduct and manner had the appearance of a constant apology for insufficiencies and mistakes he had made or was certain to make. Mr. Novotný knew himself and he had worked out a certain routine to prevent people from bawling him out or exploding at him. It was not a particularly original solution; many people find a similar one for coming to grips with their station in life and their shortcomings.

And even though he was such a little man and an intimidated one, Mr. Novotný achieved much more than building a defense system for surviving more or less satisfactorily in spite of his weaknesses and shortcomings. Mr. Novotný had ambitions, and, with all the cautiousness of a small, intimidated man, he succeeded to a certain degree in satisfying them. And that interested me very much; for that reason I tended to like him.

Mr. Novotný wanted to play a more important role than life had assigned him. At least he wanted to create that impression and use it to enjoy life, and the impression had a certain reality to it. Mr. Novotný had never hunted (except perhaps for beating the bushes as a country boy). He did not have the means. To go hunting costs money, and Mr. Novotný had to count his every penny. And perhaps because of that, he had the idea that to be a Sunday hunter must place a man in a higher social category, make him socially a more important personality. And, since he could not hunt, he satisfied himself by creating the impression that he did.

He did it in a rather original way. I have already said that he had to count his pennies. But as a civil servant he had to have an overcoat. A loden coat was quite an acceptable coat for a man of Mr. Novotný's standing. But Mr. Novotný bought himself a green loden coat, which was not a penny more expensive than another sort of coat, and the green loden coat made possible a forward step that even his little mind could conceive. By donning it, Mr. Novotný could pretend that he was a Sunday hunter. Of course, a loden coat, taken separately, was not convincing enough. Other people wore such coats, too. He needed accessories that would clearly imply to everyone that he, Mr. Novotný, belonged to the better class of people, who went hunting on Sundays. He did it rather economically, considering that he could actually play this role every day.

Mr. Novotný bought himself a hunting hat. It was the kind gamekeepers wear. He wanted to be quite certain of the impression he would create. The hat had a round, flat bottom. It was dark green with a light-green ribbon. The ribbon held a tuft of chamois bristles, which swung from side to side as he walked and drew attention to Mr. Novotný's importance. I think that the tuft was not a true chamois, but who can distinguish an imitation from the real tuft? Such people are really scarce.

But all of this did not yet satisfy Mr. Novotný. He also bought a hunting dog, and this persuaded every last doubting Thomas. It is understandable that every good dog owner walk his dog at least once a day. And that was what Mr. Novotný dutifully did. The moment he arrived home from the office and ate his late dinner, he donned his loden coat, put on his green hunting hat, and started walking his dog. Hundreds and hundreds of pedestrians took notice of the gentleman in the loden coat and thought: Here goes another Sunday hunter walking his dog. And that was exactly what pleased Mr. Novotný so much. He not only played—he actually lived—the role of a man of a higher social class. Every day he placed himself on the social ladder one or two rungs higher than where he actually stood. It was the most satisfying lifestyle he could achieve within his financial and intellectual means. It was the

30

small creative achievement of a small man in small circumstances, which appeared a little ridiculous to me and possibly does to my readers as well. But, upon closer look, it really was not that at all, not only because it evoked my sympathy and pity, but because it was in reality a solution—a personally satisfying adjustment to his conditions.

His adjustment had another advantage. Mr. Novotný not only walked his dog but also was master over him. He ordered him around, called him back, and assumed a very authoritative tone of voice. Where else could Mr. Novotný command anyone? In the office he just obeyed. And at home, I think, he obeyed too. He simply was not a man with the qualities of leadership or decision making. But with his dog he could fully play it. It pleased him, and to the pleasures of a gentleman of better circumstances was added a compensation for his feeling of inferiority.

If there were more people in this world who could find as satisfying a solution to their circumstances as did Mr. Novotný, fewer people would be neurotic and more could be happy; if all those who receive better education, who are more talented, or whose parents have influence, would show as much creativity as Mr. Novotný, many of us would lead better lives.

The End of Love

Involuntarily and unhappily, I witnessed the end of a great, lifelong devotion. Although such occurrences normally attract our avid interest, I witnessed this finale with embarrassment. I would have preferred to close my eyes, to go away, best of all to forget.

I found myself in the middle-class, comfortably appointed house almost by chance. A good friend, a violinist by profession, went to see an old friend of his, a collector of precious violins. He went to visit him often, he told me, and played some of his violins for him. It was possibly the only joy remaining to an old man of almost ninety. He had no children, his wife had died a long time ago, his eyesight and hearing were impaired, and he could no longer go out. His enjoyment of these violins, however, was a great compensation for all his life's pleasures, which had left him one after the other.

I was told all this by my friend when I met him at the house of another friend. It interested me. Besides, I was looking for a good violin for myself. Having fled my homeland, now ruled by Communists, I had no violin of my own, and played on a borrowed instrument that was not very good. My friend could see from my face how much his story intrigued me. How about coming along with him? Maybe some of the old gentleman's violins would be for sale. Of course, he loved them dearly, and it might be hard for him to part with one.

We drove to the neighboring village where everyone knew

32

the old man. While we were filling up the car, the attendant told me that the old gentleman had been bedridden for the past two months and no longer recognized anyone, not even members of his own family. My friend hesitated. Does it make any sense to visit if he would not recognize him, if he would not enjoy his playing anymore? We wanted to turn the car around when the attendant stopped us and pointed out an older woman crossing the street. That was his housekeeper, he said, and she could tell us more.

Yes, for the most part the old gentleman did not recognize anyone but he did have lucid moments. Moreover, the lady of the house, his niece, was at home and would be glad to see us. We should go ahead, she said, since we were already here. Maybe we would like some of the violins.

Both of us were very much attracted by the idea of seeing the collection of precious violins, which was now within reach, and we were glad that the housekeeper had helped us in our indecision. The niece was a middle-aged lady, who invited us inside with a resolute voice, although the old gentleman was sleeping at the moment. She said we could look at the violins. She had to return, but the housekeeper would be right back. Besides, the list of violins, with the descriptions and prices, was lying on the writing desk. Most of the violins were in the living room, and, in case we wanted to see the rest, they would be upstairs in the old gentleman's study.

The list of violins included twenty-seven instruments. One had just been sold for fifteen hundred dollars. Of course, the old gentleman actually owned forty-four instruments, we were told. Three violins were for sale in a store in a nearby town, and others were in stores in more distant places. Three violins had been given to the son of the lady of the house. The rest were free to inspect and play. All had good strings and were tuned regularly so that they could be played anytime by anyone. Most of the violins also had expensive bows.

A row of beautiful cases, mostly of leather, some of which were for two violins of the same origin, was testimony to the value of the instruments and the collector's love for them. I opened the nearest one. On the velvet lining it looked like a jewel: a carefully cleaned, polished dark red violin with new silver strings. It had been put together a year ago, by a violin maker from a neighboring town, from parts of two precious instruments, one old French and one old Italian. The combination had not been completely successful—the violin sounded wooden and hollow. An old German Weber violin had a much better tone, but I did not particularly like the rich encrustation on the top and bottom. An old French violin, by an unknown master, sounded beautiful, having a sensitive, sweet tone. Of the rest, two old French, one Italian, several old German, and about four new American handmade violins were excellent. Only one of the new American ones was still raw and had not been played long. Although the master violin maker had made it seventeen years before, only a few of the old gentleman's visitors had played it. True, some of the violins did not have balanced strings. The G string on the old Weber sounded like a French horn, but the A and E strings were much weaker.

All in all, the collection had been carefully selected. If we consider that the old gentleman himself never played the violin and that, as a former lawyer, he was only an amateur collector and violin maker (he had made a few violins), the tone of his violins showed that several violinists had advised him and that every instrument had been carefully tested and expertly judged before the old gentleman made his decision. How much loving care was in the collection! How much it meant to the old gentleman who even recently had from his bed inspected all the strings and replaced them as necessary! How many times had he carefully wiped off the resin under the bridge after some visiting violinist had played it! How often had he, in spite of his impaired hearing, tried to keep his violins tuned to the proper pitch!

The lady of the house returned. How did we like the violins? We asked about some particulars, as on the list there were apparently some contradictions. But she knew nothing about them. According to her, the old gentleman had dictated the list recently and perhaps made some mistakes, or perhaps she had made them. Besides, we had not seen the remainder of the collection upstairs. She went upstairs with my friend, but they brought down only two more. She said there were eight empty cases. Perhaps her husband had taken some to a violin dealer.

I asked which had been the most precious violin when the collection was complete. She said it was an Italian Guarneri. He himself had sold it a few years ago for four thousand dollars. He had been retired for twenty-five years and after the war had been in need of money. And what did we think of the ones that were here? Would we like some, perhaps? She would give us a small discount. The list prices were those of violin dealers. I was interested in the old French violin with the sweet mature tone. She looked at the list for a long time and then said with hesitation that she would sell it to me for twenty-five dollars less than the indicated price.

We heard a weak sound from the neighboring room. The old gentleman had just awakened. My friend was told he could go and see him. Through the open door I saw a yellow face, turned away from the light, the skin pulled tight over the bones. His eyes were almost closed, not taking in what was going on around him. He coughed, and his emaciated hand fumbled for a handkerchief. My friend entered, closing the door, while I returned to the violins. I was told I could play. He would not hear me anyway.

Before I could take the violins in my hands, junior came. A handsome, unkempt youngster, he gave me a smile but was not in the least interested in my playing. He himself was taking lessons on the smallest of the three instruments he had been given, but it did not look as if he had any interest in music.

He sat in front of the TV set and turned on a noisy murder story. At times it drowned out my playing. It was hard for me to judge the tone of the violins I was trying out. To the youngest generation, brimming with life and full of robust interest, belongs life and the future, even though it is intellectually so much poorer than the one leaving this world. Not even his great love and sophistication could help him.

My friend returned from the old gentleman's bedroom. What if we asked him about some of the violins that interested us? He might know some details. My friend only shook his head, but, before he could say anything, the lady of the house was with us again. She said that was entirely useless. He got everything mixed up, and, besides, he could not hear anything. She would tell us everything as far as the price went. I asked whether the old gentleman was aware that his violins were being sold and that we would be interested in some of them. She said he did not, that he knew nothing anymore and that it was useless to talk to him about it. But, if we liked any of them, she herself would sell them to us. She would like to hasten it while the violins were in good shape and had all the strings. When the strings gave out, the buyers would lose interest, she said. They must be in working order if they were to be sold.

In the next room the old gentleman was passing away. His love had built a great and precious collection of violins. He himself, as an amateur violin maker, repaired and maintained them. He played with them; he loved them. And in our room was an exuberant youth without the slightest understanding of this love or of the value of its objects and his mother with him, a businesswoman concerned only with a good price for the objects. Love was dying with the old gentleman; younger, more elemental and more practical interests were taking its place. When the old gentleman died his love would not be replaced with anything. All this is in the nature of things. Yet it seemed to me that, while it was there, this love should have been respected. In its passing, it should not have been interfered with either by inconsiderate youth or by business interest.

Walking in This World with Beauty

I mean with one's own beauty, not with a fairy-tale princess, with beautiful clothes, or anything similar. If someone has a beautiful appearance, he walks with it in this world all his life or at least while he is young. He cannot step out of his beautiful mien even for a short while; he cannot even for a moment play the role of an ordinary, inconspicuous person who turns nobody's head, whose beautiful appearance inspires no remarks, whom nobody envies. Yes, beauty, though it is mostly a dear and flattering quality, can sometimes be a burden. I think that beautiful people would prefer to put beauty on like a Sunday best, when they need it, when they want to charm someone, when they want to please someone. But to be beautiful all the time—Sundays and weekdays, at work or at a party, at home or in the theatre box—can be a handicap.

Beauty is a luxury, and it is not only superfluous but also out of place in nonluxurious situations. I think that in such circumstances handsome people would like to put their beauty aside for a while. And if not they themselves, then people around them, feel that it is out of place to be always so provocatively beautiful. Beauty should not be like daily bread, but like a festive dinner, not a constant quality for all situations but only for exceptional ones. It is a pity to use it—or I should say *abuse* it—when there is no need. To be beautiful doing heavy or filthy work, or while cooking, sleeping, or dealing with ugly people and other similar situations, is wholly unnecessary, perhaps even uncomfortable and unsuitable.

Of course, what I have in mind is not everyday beauty but the kind that takes your breath away when you look at it, beauty that looks like a miracle when you perceive it, beauty that makes you ask how it was possible that someone could have created it. Luckily, this uncanny admiration for extraordinary beauty usually occurs when we see a beautiful person for the first time or only infrequently. Brothers or husbands of extraordinarily beautiful women grow jaded when exposed to such grace constantly. Even though they take it in, they are not in awe of it or constantly enraptured by it. It begins to be part of everyday life. If it cannot be used only in unusual circumstances, in daily routine it changes into an ordinary thing. This only shows the need for change from the common to the unusual, from the weekday to the holiday, even though beauty remains the same. It is taken for what it is when a girl dresses in her finery, but seen as ordinary when the girl is dressed for everyday work. For people who do not see her often it is, of course, an enduring phenomenon, God's miracle, no matter what the occasion.

Many people, especially women, envy other beautiful women. They wish they could be as beautiful; they wish they could dazzle as much, be as admired and as attractive to the other sex. But in my opinion they do not know what they are asking for. I have a feeling that beauty does not bring beautiful women any happiness. I have known about five dazzling women and have followed their fate as long as possible. Beauty did not bring any of them happiness, at least not so quickly as one would expect. Beauty is something people almost fear. Young men think that a beautiful woman already has other admirers, that they are not good enough for her and that they have no hope. I can see it in watching my students. The plain girls marry easily and soon; the beauties often marry late or remain single. Perhaps the beauties are not so aggressive, because they are aware that they are attractive, and turn everyone's head, and perhaps they think that they do not have to make such an effort to gain a young man's favor.

Two of the very beautiful women whom I knew could not find a partner before their twenty-seventh year. Both women were college educated; one had a law degree. We all thought she would never marry. Almost all of her colleagues who were less endowed with beauty had long been married when we finally received her wedding announcement. We all heaved a sigh. We had all thought that it was too late for her. I do not know how happy she is in her late marriage; I have no connection with her family, and I have not seen her for years.

The second woman, even more beautiful than the first, had majored in psychology. If you looked at her closely, she seemed almost unreal. How could such beauty originate at all? And in spite of that, while she was in college, students were afraid of her. Later, when she took a position in industry, she had no luck. She herself talked to me about her bad luck. She asked me how it was that she could not get married. Not until she was twenty-six did she become engaged. We all had a feeling of relief that her bad luck had turned. In reality it was not so. Just before the wedding and after the announcement in the papers, the two separated. This was even worse luck than before. A year later there was an announcement in the paper about another marriage. But, I do not know whether this beautiful woman is happily married either.

Another, equally dazzling beauty from a very rich family was married early to an ungainly and not too clever industrialist, but hers was not a happy marriage. From the very beginning he was unfaithful to her with a number of women less beautiful than she. Her beauty was no help. Finally, she divorced him and remarried, but this marriage was not happy either. As a young girl, this beauty had only a few suitors, definitely fewer than her less attractive friends and classmates.

Equally beautiful was the daughter of a country innkeeper whom I met when she was eighteen. Not only beautiful, but with a lovely disposition, she could not marry the young man she fell in love with; his parents prevented it. Later she married a schoolteacher who was consistently unfaithful. She was very unhappy during the time I had news of her.

Another beauty I want to mention was already a middle-aged woman when I made her acquaintance; her original looks were still evident in her features and figure. How few admirers she had was evident from her marriage. She married an unsightly insurance agent. Even that could not have been a satisfactory match for reasons of status. In her career her beauty did not help either; she was a college teacher, but she rarely got a promotion and remained in the lower ranks of her profession.

Is it by chance that I never met a single dazzling woman who was married early and to a handsome, compatible man with whom she could be happy? Obviously, five examples are not enough to draw general conclusions, but it is remarkable that these five women had such fates. Their beauty intimidated suitors and when they married, failed to bring them happiness.

Great beauty is extraordinary, and people react to it in extraordinary ways. Mankind generally is not beautiful, as some animals are. Deer and eagles are all beautiful; among them beauty is no handicap. On the other hand, moose are all ugly; among them beauty cannot be found. But among people it sometimes occurs, and then it cannot find a place among the less beautiful. It remains an exception, having to bear its consequences. And these are often less than pleasant.

I Played the Representative
of the Czech King

Yes, indeed, I played the representative of the Czech king, and I did this not as a boy but as a mature man. It was serious play, not a play performed to amuse the public. My performance was unrehearsed. It was not a role but the performance of a function in the place of a Czech king. Perhaps the whole thing seems unreal because no Czech kings exist anymore, not even the imposed, uncrowned kings installed by the Hapsburgs. Yes, it is really true. We do not have a Czech king, and we did not have him even in 1945 when my role was played out. Yet there have remained certain institutions from the times of Czech kings, a host of them, which survive their times and have relevance even today when Communism rules the land of former kings.

One of these institutions is the crown of Saint Wenceslas, and with it are connected certain functions originating in the times of the Czech kingdom. Among them is the care and occasional inspection of that crown. Such an inspection took place after the defeat of Nazi Germany. Nobody knew whether the Germans had hidden it somewhere, just as they hid and stole so many historical relics. It was imperative to make certain whether the crown was still in its place. Inspections of the crown of Saint Wenceslas are rare occurrences, with decades usually passing between them.

In a sense, the inspection is a complicated affair: a number of dignitaries have to meet to get to the crown at all. It is deposited in a special cache built especially for it in the cellar of the castle in Prague. The cache is not like the safes in a modern bank vault; those are of stainless steel, while this one is of brick, and, while the walls are very thick, they are not impregnable. Yet it gives adequate protection to this national treasure. It is in an old box, but probably not from the Middle Ages.

Access to the crown is possible only with the consent of seven dignitaries, among whom are the mayor, the archbishop of Prague, and, in earlier times, the king. Each one of these dignitaries is the keeper and guardian of one key. They have to decide on the date and hour, convene at the castle, and open the cache with all seven keys; should one of them be absent, the box could not be opened.

The keys themselves make an unusually solemn impression. They are large and richly ornamented with enamel. The locksmith's work is decorative, done by a master of his craft. One of the keys is in the possession of the Province of Bohemia. I do not like to use the expression "Province of Bohemia," because for centuries it was an illustrious kingdom; it became a kingdom several hundred years before Bavaria, Saxony, Prussia, Würtemberg, and others.

After World War II, the Province of Bohemia was governed by a newly created National Committee. Its president was Ladislav Kopřiva, a simple man, and through his political convictions very much uninvolved in the royal past of Bohemia. When the National Committee received a request for the president to appear at the castle with the key, he was unimpressed; to act as a representative of the Czech king or possibly as his chancellor, did not appeal to his Communist soul. He asked me if I, as the vice-president of the Committee, would want to take part in the ceremonial inspection of the crown. I accepted his offer with pleasure and enthusiasm.

We all gathered at the castle on time and descended the very old wooden stairs into the cellar. All keys opened the locks easily. Professor Matějíček, who was present as an expert, opened the door to the box and took out a round container with the crown. It had the appearance of very strong cardboard, quite worn at the top, although in reality, of course, it was not. Although the container was very old, I cannot make the remotest guess about its age. Professor Matějíček carefully took the crown out. For me it was a very solemn occasion. I had never seen the crown of Saint Wenceslas, although I believe it had been publicly exhibited.

The crown is of solid gold, and, as is well known, it is decorated with a great number of precious stones of unusual size. But that was not what impressed me most. I was overwhelmed by the realization that this crown had been held successively by all the Czech kings over a period of six hundred years. An expert could perhaps discover on its surface the fingerprints of Charles IV, Wenceslas IV, George of Poděbrady, Vladislav, or other Czech kings. But, if they were found, of course, who would know what Charles IV's fingerprints looked like?

One after the other, we took the crown into our hands. When I took it I gave it my undivided and excited attention. Involuntarily I added my fingerprints to those of the Czech kings. I felt a bond between me and them, both spiritual and physical. With my fingers and eyes I reached deeply into the Czech past, not only into the history of Czech lands but also of its highest representatives. In those few seconds were joined the six hundred years of Bohemia—from the founding of the kingdom to the newest Communist invention of the National Committee. I was one of the links that successively represented the highest political authority of Bohemia. I had a feeling of humility before the long chain of historical personages, before the grandeur of all things this crown had represented for six hundred years, before the grandeur of Czech history.

I had been, of course, familiar with this grandeur and time span. But facts are not everything. The question is how we experience them. During the moment I held the crown of Saint Wenceslas in my hand, I had a new, profound understanding of these facts. I cannot even say that I was moved or fascinated. It was something much more serious and responsible. I was bound by new bonds to my country. I felt the sanctity of these bonds. I grew new roots into the past of the Czech kingdom.

The other participants were, I think, calmer than I. Jan Masaryk made jokes, as usual, and Professor Matějíček discussed the artistic and technical aspects of the goldsmith's work. The rest looked quiet and matter-of-fact. I think such behavior is rather the rule than the exception. We pass by great things without breaking stride, and the greatness of unusual happenings strikes us only years after. In the inspection of the crown of Saint Wenceslas, I was endowed with more interest and more sensitivity than the rest. And I am grateful for it.

Birdwatchers*

I use the English expression not only because Czech has no equivalent but also because it refers to something typical of Anglo-Saxon countries. Usually in groups, "birdwatchers" observe birds during their mating season, during nesting, feeding, migrating to faraway lands, and at any other time; everything that the various kinds of birds do and the way they behave, interests them and evokes their enthusiasm. In the United States, birdwatching is a widespread, well-organized movement.

Birdwatching is, I would say, a crossroads of several modern cultural values and perhaps some innate interests of man. In my youth, I myself had a strong interest in nature and still have it. As a student, I watched birds and animals; I collected beetles and butterflies. I remember how excited I always was when I found a species I had not seen before or when I saw an especially beautiful specimen of one I knew already. I did not go after normal specimens of species I knew and possessed already. My interest was different from that of birdwatchers: I cannot say that it was a scientific interest yet, since it was just a youthful one.

Well, what is a scientific interest in nature? First of all, a scientist knows all the established species. Occasionally he

*Translator's note: This word was in English in the original.

46

may succeed in finding an entirely new species; describing it is a very satisfying experience. This is a very rare and unusual occurrence and it happens only to a few individuals once or twice in a lifetime. Otherwise the scientist studies the known species calmly, rationally and expertly, showing a special interest in them, be it the influence of the environment, heredity, mutations, or changes of habitat. He is a rationalist, a creative scientific worker, one who takes an objective attitude toward his subject. Of course, at heart he loves his subject, but he does not feel sentimental toward individual specimens, and thus he is basically different from the type of people who observe birds in the special way that constitutes birdwatching.

There is yet another strong current in modern man's interest in nature. It is Romanticism. Around the year 1800, in opposition to enlightened Rationalism, there came to life first a literary and then a middle-class current of emotional appreciation of elements of nature. The fragrance and shadows of the woods, the ruggedness and inaccessibility of the mountains, the beauty of wild flowers, all of this the Romantics experienced with deeply felt emotions. A Romantic was not interested in looking for unknown species, in understanding nature rationally, or in examining known kinds of birds or flowers. Birds of the woods were merely a charming decoration with their songs, flitting about, with their colors and games, be they robins, cardinals, thrushes, or finches. There was no interest in separating and identifying species; the interest was global, cumulative, and above all esthetic. Nature as a whole was a source of enthusiasm; any search for scientific laws or the use of precise descriptions did not belong in the period, in a direct contradiction to the Romantic concept of nature.

There is another, very extensive outlook on nature. It is that of the people who make their living in nature: farmers, gamekeepers, fishermen. They see nature first of all as their source of livelihood. But that is not all. Their interest is practical and materialistic, but they too love nature—except they are not enthusiasts. Even the farmer appreciates the song of the lark and likes to look at the field of grain waving in the wind, but he is not a dreamer. He is someone who loves his work and everything that belongs to it. He does not search for profound emotional experiences in nature and, of course, does not write poetry about it.

Well, then, to which cultural type do birdwatchers belong? Very clearly to none of them. Nor do they belong to yet another type I have not mentioned—the housewife who cultivates flowers in her windowsill pots. She nurtures them from seeds, watches their growth, enjoys them, and admires the lovely colors, which are the goal, as it were, of her cultivation. Here belong amateur gardeners, too. Enjoying the result of their work, they admire beautifully developed specimens and, more than the housewife, try to know all the species of the flowers that grow in their garden. The joy of these people is in the creation; it is the joy of their own work or that of their friends. Behind each well-developed flower they see above all the labor that someone devoted to it. Yet, amateur gardeners are enthusiastic about garden flowers but not about wildflowers; they have a lively interest in them, but they do not possess a real scientific preoccupation.

Birdwatchers are on the one hand a combination of some of these cultural types and on the other they are in a class of their own. First of all, they are partly romantics. They are entranced with uncultivated nature but only with a small part of it, for they are interested only in birds. As opposed to the real romantics, they want to know the individual species, their characteristics, and behavior. In this they resemble scientists, and in fact they draw their knowledge from scientific handbooks. But they do not strive for deeper scientific understanding or new discoveries; they are satisfied with what is already known. Unlike ornithologists and like the romantics, they take

48

undiluted pleasure in every repeated experience. If today they see a certain kind of a woodpecker pecking at a tree, they aim their binoculars at him and enjoy watching him. If they see him a week later, they enjoy him just as much. And, if they see some unusual species, they are enthralled, even though it has been known for a long time and even though it is probably very common in other lands. In this they resemble collectors: the rarer something is, the greater the pleasure. Scientists do not value rarity to that extent.

Birdwatchers certainly do not belong among those who work in nature, such as farmers, gardeners, or foresters. They accept nature as it is; they enjoy it like romantics, and try to understand it like scientists. They are not interested in nature as a source of impressions, which makes them different from the romantics, and they do not spread the knowledge of nature, which makes them different from scientists. Aside from these two cultural types, they have in them a little bit of another type I have not mentioned: the Chinese mandarins. It is said that the mandarins could without moving observe their goldfish for hours. They knew what the fish would do; they knew their habits and were pleased when they observed what they already knew; of course, they were also breeders, which the birdwatchers are not.

Birdwatchers are then a type unto themselves even though they have the qualities of other cultural types. Like all the others, birdwatchers draw the strength of their experiences and interests from other people, for birdwatching is usually done in groups; people draw one another's attention to what they see and share their joy and interest. A member receives not only factual information but also some of the delight and adds a little to the joy of others. If the group is larger, a very normal group enthusiasm develops, and part of it remains forever in the emotional makeup of the participants. In the course of time, the group forms its own special emotions, which hold it together and which make the members apostles of their movement and its faithful adherents.

Birdwatching definitely has its place in modern life, which has lost so much with the decline of religious feeling, with haste and with the monotony of industrial products. It fills a gap in the emotional life of modern man in a manner that is positive, agreeable, and definitely healthful.

A Life of Devotion

There are many selfish people. Everyone says so. Some even claim that selfish people are in the majority, or that everyone is selfish; others are merely convinced that selfish people are growing in number. I do not know what to think of such opinions. First of all, there is, of course, no reliable way to measure selfishness, and then some people can be selfish in certain situations (for instance in their employment) and unselfish in others (perhaps toward their children). Be that as it may, there certainly are unselfish people, even some who are incredibly unselfish. I know several, and I pay more attention to them than to the others. They are beautiful exceptions in this admittedly selfish word; they warm our hearts and give us faith that life can be beautiful.

I have in mind one such man especially. He held a position in a political party and at one time served as my personal secretary. We have known each other for years and lived through many events together, so I could observe him closely and over a long period of time and find out what kind of a man he really was; I knew him both at home and in exile.

This friend of mine remained single, being too devoted to the political party he served; he had time only for the party, leaving no energy or time for marriage. He gave the party the time and energy that remained to him after work. Of course, you may say that there are many people like that. They are so filled with ambition, they endeavor so feverishly to make a political career that they shove everything else aside. But here is the big difference: my friend did not strive for a political career. He wanted only to serve; he wished to live for something, he wanted to be devoted to something other than himself. He had to cling to something impersonal, to something that would have greater meaning than materialistic goals and he wanted to serve that ideal.

In this way he served as a local functionary of our mutual political party for years without achieving any paid public office. He was not interested in that; he had a need to serve, and in this way he found fulfillment. Had there not been a political party, he would have found something else.

What was remarkable in his case was that he did serve a political party. As you all know, a party is a hotbed of ambitions, career hunting, and personal interests. And in this atmosphere he remained unselfish and devoted to the cause. If I say that he was like a rose among thorns, it is not enough. He was like a white sheep among black ones, like a white water-lily in dirty water.

His devotion was in reality twofold, or maybe threefold. He was devoted to the party as a political organization, to its leaders and to its program. All of these were sacred to him, and he served all of them faithfully and devotedly. His great goal in life was to serve well; food and drink, erotic interests, functions and positions, reward and glory, power and influence—all these were secondary to him. He never looked at a problem in his personal life from these viewpoints, in spite of so many people around him doing just that. I do not even know how this was possible. He saw personal ambition all around him; he even advised some of his political friends how to achieve higher positions, but he never acted on such advice himself. It was as if he were aware that it was all right for the others but not for him, as if rules valid for the others were different from those valid for him. He went so far as to mask his unselfishness with a certain brusqueness so that nobody would see through it.

Of course, in our party, many people were devoted to the cause. Many made sacrifices, served faithfully and with conviction. I even think that we had more such people than the other parties, although I cannot prove it statistically, and I judge my party perhaps more favorably because I was one of its members. But none of these party faithfuls was completely indifferent to public functions, to satisfaction of personal ambitions, to personal interests. Even though they did not emphasize them, these were at least their secondary motives; in other words, they were not entirely without such interests.

My friend was. Of course, even he achieved certain paid and unpaid positions. He was very useful to the party serving in them, and so he took them and performed them well. But he considered them only as a service to the party. Such was his concept of them in contrast to the ordinary party members.

This very striking exception is quite unusual in the framework of a modern party. Other institutions may have more such people. Scientists have their sacred cow—their scientific specialty, which they serve to the detriment of their family's financial interests. Saints have lived only for God, and there are missionaries who sacrifice their personal lives to preach Christian ideals. But even these people have their selfish satisfaction. The scientist achieves recognition, the satisfaction of discovery or perhaps only a more mundane goal—a full professorship; the saint and the missionary perhaps achieve everlasting fame and a place near God. Besides, these devoted people live in an environment that nourishes and supports their devotion and service to an ideal. Then, of course, there are people such as Dr. Albert Schweitzer. These people in part are like the missionaries, in part of a special breed.

My friend had nothing of the character of scientists, saints, or missionaries; he never expected recognition or reward, either

53

in this world or in the life hereafter. And he was in a profession in which the rewards of a scientist or a saint are not forthcoming. He would belong, actually, to the category of special people, even though he differed from Dr. Schweitzer and those like him in a very substantial way. He was special because he needed to serve something, something that had not been defined beforehand. It had to be, of course, something in which he believed, something which he accepted positively and regarded as worthy of his devotion.

This was apparent also in exile. The party had ceased to exist. From the secretary to a vice-chairman of the government, he became an exile looking for work. He found a modest job as a janitor in a private school. And again he served the school body and soul. Although he did not know English, he was usually liked by the youngsters, teachers, and the administration. They trusted him so much that, when he had to retire at the age of sixty-five, they let him have the keys to the school building. In his free time, he visited the school and saw to it that everything was in order. This he did for a number of years. In the meantime he secured work as a cashier in a business firm. Here also he became a devoted employee, even though he could not quite identify with the goals of the firm, which were more materialistic than idealistic.

Although the party did not continue to exist in exile, its leaders were here. And to them my friend continued his devotion, and performed—and still performs—many valuable services. He regularly calls the former chairman of the party on the telephone, although they live in different cities and this is quite expensive for him. My friend will continue to be devoted to his first love till the end. Such is usually the case with any great love.

And now, how is it possible to understand all of this? I am not quite certain. But it seems to me that to my friend the party was a substitute for a lover, a wife, and children. He did not marry and did not have children. But he had to love something, live for something, be devoted to something. This need was perhaps stronger in him than in other people, but it was not fulfilled, as it is in most people. He turned it to something that was accessible. Most people, of course, do not have such a need for devotion, at least to such a degree. But those, who have it and find an object worthy of their devotion, are, I think, happier than those seeking only personal, selfish goals. I think that even my friend found much happiness in his devotion to the party. Everyone who knew him wished him well.

On the other hand, many ambitious people who sought positions and careers, and achieved them, were not as happy as he was. Why do people look for happiness in a doubtful enterprise and overlook areas in which it is rather easily obtainable? Of course, these people do not have such an unselfish need for devotion and service. I congratulate anyone who has it.

Unnecessary Activity

Normally people are inclined to work less rather than more. Labor unions constantly press for shorter working hours and instruct their members to work less. They consider "feather-bedding" an essential part of their political mission. They also try to lengthen summer vacations. All this is partly because people are not anxious to work, partly to cut down on unemployment. On the other hand, independent people whose income depends on how much they work, such as many doctors, lawyers, businessmen, and others, sometimes devote fourteen to sixteen hours a day to their work. Of course, we cannot say that they do it gladly; they force themselves to work in order to gain more money.

There are only a few people who work hard because they like it. They are full of energy, and dissipate their excess energy through work. It gives them pleasure. Then there are people who are devoted to an idea: researchers, preachers, apostles of a new idea, inventors and other inspired idealists. There are only a few. The rule is the less work, the better; the tendency to work the least possible is considered natural.

It was a shock, then, the other day, when I was about to buy a thermometer. The salesclerk opened a drawer in which there were perhaps fifty or more thermometers of the same type. I was surprised that they did not all show the same temperature but had differences of up to two degrees. That was disconcerting, and I did not know which thermometer to take. It seemed to me that the most exact one would show a temperature between the two extremes. I started looking for such a thermometer, when it occurred to me that all those thermometers were actually indicating temperature all the time. Of course, this has to be, especially when the store is open: It wouldn't do for a thermometer to stop showing temperature the moment a customer bought one, for he would refuse to buy it. Thermometers must show the temperature when the store is open. But what about when it is closed? Then of course it no longer matters, and thermometers can do as they please. Nobody forces them to work when the store is closed. Let them rest! But, strangely enough, thermometers do not. They measure the temperature with an almost incredible perseverance whether people want them to or not. All fifty thermometers in that one drawer work without rest, without relief, without concern that the others are doing the same thing. Such useless activity, such pointless ardor! Can't they make an agreement among themselves? Can't they come to an understanding, can't they get organized? They are all together, in one place! Nothing would be easier than to take turns. To show the same temperature fifty times or more is just plain nonsense.

But thermometers are not people. Not only can they not organize themselves into a union, as people do; they do not even want to, and, moreover, they are unable to stop showing temperature. It is a necessity, part of their physical nature. And, in spite of that, when a person opens such a drawer with fifty thermometers, something strikes him. One does not do such useless work. It is not customary and it is even against common sense. People are not only lazy; they are also rational. Thermometers are not. They cannot conceive what is useless and irrational.

At first I thought that the nature of thermometers was better than that of people. It would certainly be different if people worked as willingly as thermometers. Of course, people are rational and would limit all this useless activity. If only people had willingness and inclination for work! How different everything would be! How much more could we give to the poor and needy! How many more hospitals and schools could be built! How much bigger the gross national product! How much better off we would be! And yet these thoughts are obsolete today. If we worked this way, we would have no need for automation. Not only that, we would not even be able to use it, nor have the interest to invent it.

So it seems that human aversion to work and plain laziness are good for something. They force us to think of saving labor, of achieving more with less effort. And we succeed. We create inventions, ever more inventions, mainly so that machines can work for us and we can work less. And this has the added advantage that much more is achieved than if we toiled and invented nothing. Thermometers are therefore not a fitting example for man. Let us be thankful that we are not thermometers. Let us even be glad that we are people with a tendency toward laziness. And yet, if you open a drawer full of thermometers, something moves you, but moves you only because our attention is directed toward people and their problems. For the same reason we anthropomorphize living and nonliving things and compare them to people: Dogs are more faithful than people, cats more elegant, thermometers more diligent. But what is the use of such comparisons? We possess our unique intelligence, and that compensates for almost everything; with it, we are ahead of everything else. Therefore, long live people, with all their tendency toward laziness! They are the only creatures who make good use of it.

Walking on Two Crutches

I mean it figuratively, and yet what comes to mind is the literal meaning when I speak either English or Czech. I have been away from home for so long that I am slowly losing the certainty and the richness of expression of my mother tongue. And not only that, some English expressions seem so handy and of such happy coinage that I am inclined to use them even when I talk Czech. Some indeed express an idea better than Czech ones, but, of course, there are many Czech expressions that are better than English ones. But I have no intention of discussing the advantages and maturity of these two languages; I want only to point out what happens when an exile uses them after a lengthy stay abroad. I want to show how poor and culturally crippled he is.

When I arrived in America I already knew English, but only in the way I might put a child's puzzle together or play a French king in an amateur stage production. I had mastered English systematically; I could put words together fairly well, and every once in a while I enjoyed using them idiomatically. It was all conscious; it was a kind of intellectual game. My relations with people and objects, my attitudes toward them and ways of understanding them, were Czech; my thoughts were formed by Czech expressions and Czech phraseology. In reality I silently translated Czech ideas, formed by the Czech language, into English. To Americans, it must have seemed artificial and awkward, but it generally served its purpose.

Sometimes, of course, it did not. I would say that someone was "a very sympathetic person" and mean that he felt sympathy toward people and not, as in Czech, that he evokes affection in them. But the connection was good enough to make understanding possible. Or I would say "just a second," which is quite understandable, although I must have appeared to the Americans to be very fast. They prefer to say "just a minute," even when they think that they will do something in a much shorter time.

In short, I used English the way a lame man uses crutches. I helped myself by constructing phrases I knew well from my mother tongue, and used them as crutches in order to make myself understood in English. And one never walks on crutches as smoothly and as fast as on one's own healthy legs. But what can a foreigner do? It is much better to limp in a foreign language than not to walk on foreign soil at all.

Of course, I did not realize how clumsy and amusing it sometimes sounds until a few days ago when I talked with an American of Czech descent who was born in the United States. He was looking for a document for me and wanted to say (in Czech): "If I could only find the document!" And he said the equivalent of: "If I could only lay my hands on it!" A Czech native would think: "Well, then, what good would it do to put your hands on it? What purpose would it serve? What else could you do but take them off it again?" Similar thoughts must occur to Americans when they hear English spoken by a Czech who has learned the language from books. Of course, Americans do not analyze as much, nor are they as caustic or scornful as we. They do not think as much about unimportant things; they think more about practical problems, and the stream of their ideas is slow and interrupted.

But what does it matter if a person's speech sounds clumsy and maybe even ridiculous in a foreign language! What matters is to master one's own language. A man should be absolute master of one single language, which gives him a rich network of concepts and expressions with which to seize the reality around him with acrobatic certainty, firmness, joyful virtuosity, and masterful clarity. Yes, you may think that these statements are exaggerated. Those of you who have lived only at home do not realize that your language ability has all of these qualities. But after years in a foreign country, one feels it very convincingly. It is like an old man remembering how physically and mentally strong he was when he was young. But in his youth he never thought about it. It was a matter of course.

To walk at home with a flexible and firm step, without crutches, and in a foreign land with one crutch is not so bad. It is more or less natural, and one can live with it. You are an ordinary man; you feel like the eagle who can fly superbly but must walk awkwardly on the ground. What of it? It is natural and quite sufficient.

But take the case of a man who has lived in the United States and worked among Americans for ten or more years, a man who speaks Czech at home, occasionally reads a Czech book and frequents other Czechs. How many foreign words creep into his Czech! He may replace some at the last minute by the right Czech expression, but others he may not manage to replace fast enough, and will use the English. Other times, he will express his thought in Czech, but it will only be a loose translation from English. He corrupts his mother tongue with English.

What is the good of all this? He is not master of his own language anymore. Gone is all the joyousness, readiness, and certainty. And there is much more involved than that. A language is not just words but also concepts, through which to perceive reality. They are like a net that we throw on reality to be able to manipulate it (in Henri Bergson's words). Language also means complex expressions, turns of phrase, and figurative expressions. It is part of our culture, which is incomplete and partly inaccessible when we do not master our language fully.

And what is more, a language is part of our personality, a means to grasp and express what is going on inside us. We live our lives more fully if we speak and write our own language well. We are culturally alive only when we master our language easily and perfectly. That's why it gives us pleasure to speak well and to the point, whether only relating an anecdote or speaking in public. Language is an instrument of our own personality, an instrument of its life, its fullness, and a source of life's contentment.

The man who does not master at least one language fully is a lame man. He has to help himself with a gesture, a smile, a look on his face, and he has to leave a lot of his inner life unsaid. He moves slowly, with difficulty, and does not go far. He is like a man walking with a crutch; the crutch helps but does not replace healthy legs.

Well, then, you will say, when you slowly forget your mother tongue, you are slowly but certainly learning the foreign language. That is certainly true. But rest assured that you will never learn the foreign language perfectly, not even if you could live in the foreign country for a hundred years. Only children and youngsters succeed in doing it. And even then something from their mother tongue often remains in their newly acquired language. And if they want to learn the other language to perfection, they have to devote themselves to it, read and talk a lot, and even then seldom do they become masters.

At first, the exile in his bilingual surroundings limps heavily on one leg. He uses his crutch more than is necessary. Slowly he adjusts, and his limping becomes less noticeable. Maybe, if he is careful, he may almost manage to walk straight at times, but he remains in his newly accepted country a cultural and linguistical toddler. On the other hand, his healthy, sophisticated, and culturally refined Czech slowly languishes, loses its firmness and strength, and needs more and more support. The exile uses a crutch for the other leg, too; he does not walk smoothly, jauntily, or securely—even in his own tongue.

From the standpoint of language and, of course, culture, after some years the exile becomes a man on two crutches. He is an incomplete and not quite healthy personality. He limps on both legs and no longer knows the joy of an elegant and flowing gait, let alone skipping, running, or even dancing. Something is missing in his own tongue and even more so in his newly acquired language. Only the lifegiving atmosphere of his old homeland would cure him. Otherwise he is doomed to limp till the end of his life.

Our Misha

Actually I should say Hanička's Misha, because Misha belonged to her. But we soon grew so fond of Misha that we all considered him ours. At the end, which in human terms was tragic, we were all without exception crushed. We could not hold back our tears, and even today we cannot overcome a feeling of deep suffering and irrevocable loss.

Far from being exaggerated, all this is understated, even though Misha was just a little animal. He was so tiny that we could carry him in the pocket of a shirt or a blouse or hold him in the palm of our hand. How dear it was to feel his warm little body and the fast beats of his little heart! Misha was a kind of hamster brought to the United States from somewhere in Asia Minor. To all of us he was a beloved friend or rather a member of the family, coddled and petted much as the youngest children in the family are.

Every evening Misha would get a carefully prepared supper in his own little dish. It consisted of five or more of his favorite courses, always including a little bit of salami, smoked ham or chicken, a little bit of cheese, usually one grape or one blueberry, two or three kernels of cooked corn, two to three pieces of spaghetti, a little bit of cottage cheese, and such. In the second little dish we put fresh water. Toward ten o'clock in the evening he would look for his dish of food, and, when he found it, he immediately started eating. Often we added a little bit of what we just happened to be eating. Misha knew right away which food he would eat first and which would follow. It was incredible how quickly he made a decision. Once he decided he would not eat a certain food, he did not take even the least bit, even though we tried to encourage him. He simply pretended not to see it and walked around it as if it were not there. This immediacy, clarity, and steadfastness of decision impressed us greatly. In this respect, cats often behave just the other way. They stare, hesitate and often only after a long while do they decide for or against something.

Mishka was of a gentle and quiet nature. Even though at first he dodged when we petted him, he moved away slowly and somehow tactfully. Later he dodged less and less, and in the end he let us pet him quite patiently and amicably. Only twice, during the two years we had him, did he revolt. It was in his youth when he was not yet used to us and did not understand us. Before we had bought a cage for Mishka, we did not know where to put him. At night he would run out of his box and most often he would hide in the couch which we had to take apart to find him. Therefore, for the time being, we put him in the bathtub, the sides of which he could not climb. Yet he tried it, and innumerate times he climbed the smooth walls of the tub only to slide back down again and again. This lasted for hours, and in the end Mishka was exhausted and very upset. At the time someone in the family (I no longer remember who) wanted to take him out of the tub, and the frightened Mishka bit him a little. It did not amount to much. It seemed to us that, even in his upset state, he did not want to hurt anyone. This was repeated again later under different circumstances. The bite was again negligible; not a bit of blood showed. And yet Mishka had the strong teeth of a rodent and he certainly was capable of inflicting a deep wound. But evidently he did not want to hurt us.

Mishka's defensive attitude was also apparent in other ways. When we stroked him, he lowered his body as far as he could, but he did not run away and did permit us to pet him. I liked to touch his paperthin ears, something that he did not like at all. He usually bent his ears back flat against his head so that I could not take them into my hand. But both of these ways of resisting became less and less pronounced, and in the end he allowed us to fully enjoy stroking him and me to touch his paper ears.

Mishka's end was unexpected. The night before he died, he was very lively, and there was nothing the matter with him. He undoubtedly died because the temperature in the car where we left him was too high. It must have been between 130° and 140°, and Mishka could not possibly have survived. This was our fatal mistake, our great guilt. We were so tired walking along the streets of Williamsburg that we forgot about Mishka. There were so many interesting things to see. We kept wanting to see more and more until it was too late. We should think of the ones we love and who are in our care. We were guilty of having been so entranced by historical monuments that Mishka's fate escaped our attention.

We can find a slight but insufficient excuse in two extenuating circumstances: When we placed Mishka in the car in the morning, it was cool. Later it got gradually warmer until it was really hot. Second, we had left Mishka in the car often, especially when we were traveling, and he always survived. Of course, it was usually on cold days and always for a short time, never for so long as in Williamsburg. And never before had it gotten hot so quickly and without warning. These mitigating circumstances of course do not acquit us of guilt. We had done wrong to Mishka, and we feel our guilt very deeply. Rightfully we have bitter pangs of conscience, and rightfully we shall probably never overcome them.

It was about five hours before we remembered Mishka, and then it took a while for us to reach him. That was decidedly too long; Mishka could not possibly have survived. When we finally returned to the car, I unlocked the doors fast and quickly opened them wide. An immense heat enveloped me. In spite of all my anxiety and fear, I hesitated to look into Mishka's cage. The terrible heat in the car was an ominous sign of Mishka's fate. I had the feeling that I could not stand the heat even for a minute. How could tiny Mishka have endured it? My wife was the first who, driven by worry about Mishka, had the courage to open the cage and take him into her hand. As everyone waited, quietly tense, she took the immobile Mishka out. I cried out, as if to deny what had happened. I did not want to accept the terrible fact that Misha was dead—and through our negligence at that. It was simply unacceptable. Involuntarily I spoke to him: "Oh, no, no, Mishka!" Hanička started sobbing.

Our next reaction was disbelief in his death. We somehow wanted to persuade ourselves that Mishka only felt faint because of the heat. But in reality, though he was still warm (it was that hot in the car), Mishka was already stiff. He must have died quite some time earlier.

We had to leave. We sat in the car without a word. My wife took Mishka into both her hands. Maybe subconsciously she felt that her care and love would somehow help him. We left Williamsburg in a sort of panic-stricken grief. Yara kept holding Misha in her hand in the vague hope that maybe he was still alive after all. As I now understand it, there was another reason for holding him. It was a sort of last fondling and it was a last homage to him.

We covered a few miles and nothing changed. We were quiet—Mishka was also quiet—and we tried to suppress our tears. Hanička and Jiřinka cried openly. It became clearer to us that Misha would not come to life again and that we had to bury him. We wanted to stop somewhere near a forest and dig a dignified grave for him. But no place seemed appropriate to us, and the search became too long for me. I had too much tension in me. In my grief, which would not go away, I stopped near a sand dune. Without asking anyone, I jumped out, opened my fishing knife, and began to dig. I had to do something for Misha, something that would somehow help him—even if only toward eternal rest. Yara maintained that we should probably look for another place, somewhere in the forest, but, driven by grief, bitterness and guilt that I had to get rid of or at least mitigate, I kept digging fast and with a decisiveness that was incomprehensible to me.

When the little grave was dug, I took Misha in my hand for a while and turned him toward me in order to see the long rodent teeth, which we always wanted to examine but which he did not like to show; then I put him quickly into the little pit. Just as fast I covered him with sand.

Since Misha had been irrevocably taken away from us, I had to perform the burial ceremony as fast as possible and quickly get behind the wheel and drive on! I had to drive away from all this, away from taking leave of Mishka, who was our small helpless ward, our collective and personal joy. He had been part of our home, a living member of the family.

With our growing physical distance from Mishka's grave, symbolizing the final separation from Mishka, there was renewed crying. Never in our lives would we be near him again. Never would we return to the place where he was buried. It was many hundreds of miles from our home. And even if we wanted to, we would never find his grave. There were so many similar places along the road! And what would be the use? It would not bring Mishka back.

Even though I quickly got into the car and started to drive, as if I wanted to run away from grief, I did not drive fast. What good would it do to reach our destination twenty minutes earlier? Why pass other cars as was my habit? Or why drive at all? Was it not a matter of indifference and insignificant in view of our loss? Did it matter at all?

About thirty miles down the road we stopped at a gas station. I bought gas and oil and went to wash my hands. I realized that only a while ago my hand had held Mishka for the last time. Something of Mishka was left on them. It was the last of my physical contact with him. This I now washed off with the soap of an unknown gas station owner, who had no idea that at his place I buried our dear Mishka for the second time. Mishka left my life physically, completely and with finality; it was the breaking of the last physical ties. But not of other ties. I remained emotionally attached to him. He remained as dear to me as before.

Many times I asked myself how it was possible that we had grown so emotionally attached to Mishka. How can one explain that man can become so fond of an animal that it is sometimes dearer to him than another human or even a close friend? I cannot explain it and my earlier attempts at an explanation were certainly mistaken or incomplete. Psychologists certainly do not understand it, and social psychologists do not fare any better. For me, it was surprising. I had never had a pet before. I did not realize what a great capacity for loving an animal exists in man. Many people do not realize it. They are surprised when they find it in someone, especially in spinsters.

I can only comprehend and say what I especially liked about Misha. But his charming characteristics did not add up to what I am trying to understand—love for Misha. That was stronger than the sum total of his qualities and perhaps was not even dependent on them. The love was an entity. It was like one rich flower, growing from a stem, which we never saw. We only know that it had moisture, sunshine, air, and other conditions, but it certainly also grew from further inner causes, out of the strength of the human soul.

I know that Mishka was dear to us because he was so tiny. We saw him as a very diminished human being, as it were. He had tiny paws which he exercised and manipulated as a man moves his hands. They even were pink, almost like human hands. He held food in them almost in the same way as humans do. Of course, most of the things he grasped were disproportionately large, and he held them with both paws. He held a grape the same way a man would hold a basketball or a melon.

Misha also washed and scrubbed himself the way people do. He washed his little face very systematically and diligently. I cannot understand very well how he knew that he was dirty and what degree of cleanliness he wanted to achieve with his scrupulous washing, but it endeared him to our hearts. He also stored food. I know it is an instinct that rodents of his type have. But to us it seemed as if he had a human worry for the future and anticipated bad times to come. He stored food first in the pockets of his cheeks, and later stored it in another, less visible place. He had several such caches. It seemed to us that often he forgot where his storage place was because the next day he would hide food in another place. Of course, we may have confused him because the kitchen counter, which he roamed at night, was often cleaned and boxes and other things were rearranged.

It was also charming the way Misha did not realize that we were taking care of him and that there would always be enough food for him. Of course, Misha could not know that he had "tenure" in our house, that we would always take care of him and feed him, even if we did not have enough ourselves. In reality he was not all that simpleminded when he stored food for bad times to come.

All these and some other qualities made Misha a dear companion to us, a small and at the same time great friend. But the most important quality was one I have not yet mentioned. Misha never did anything out of spite, and, when he grew to maturity, he never did anything against us. Even when he did not like something, he put up with it or slowly and tactfully bent his body away. This is a rare quality, which we do not often find in people. We took it to mean respect or even devotion. Where does such a quality originate? How is it possible that people, even good people, are much less perfect in this regard than a tiny animal without any upbringing? From infancy children resist many of their parents' wishes and continue even as adults. Upbringing may even encourage such resistance.

It is possible that in a few cases upbringing spoils the human capacity for love. For most people, love remains untouched even if it is undeveloped, as through repeated disappointments or lack of love. Love can blossom even in very gruff and hard individuals provided they have the opportunity. Mishka gave us such an opportunity, and we are grateful to him. He gave it to us in rich and full measure without being aware of it. Do you understand how people sometimes have to be grateful to animals? Do you understand that there is actually something to be grateful for? Do you understand that this can make the most beautiful quality people are capable of? Goodbye, Mishka, and thanks, many thanks.

Forced Acquaintance

I am not thinking of a young girl of the nineteenth century whose strict father chose a suitable bridegroom and forced her to accept the suitor's formal visit, bouquet in hand, and later his offer of marriage. Such things do not happen anymore. I have nothing romantic in mind. There are so many other ways we can be forced to make someone's acquaintance. As a young man, when I started to work for the State Bureau of Statistics, I had to make the acquaintance of my superior, of the colleague with whom I shared my office, of the head of the department, the president of the Bureau, my subordinates, and many other people. There was no way out. And I had to look polite and amiable. That was the condition of being hired, keeping my job, and eventually being promoted.

It is equally necessary for a lawyer to make the acquaintance of his clients, for a physician of his patients. We must, or almost must, make the acquaintance of our neighbors, just as we must get to know the young men or women our children marry. As pupils, we have to get to know our teachers.

These are merely samples of a few situations in which we must make someone's acquaintance. According to the rules of the Western culture, we have to carry it out in a decent, polite manner, often kindly and joyfully. All these meetings take place face-to-face, mostly with a handshake and a smile. Those about to be acquainted stand close to each other, sometimes very close. All those ways of getting acquainted have been with us for hundreds of years.

But physical proximity is not the condition of making an acquaintance. People who correspond for their firm with someone in Africa or Australia also get acquainted. High school students whose class decides to correspond with the same grade in Japan make still closer acquaintances. They inform the others about their school, the subjects they are taking, their interests, the games they play, their parents and siblings, what they would like to become when they grow up, and similar things. Physically they remain distant and, at best, know each other from photographs.

There are other ways of making an acquaintance, by nature new, brought about by modern inventions. When I accepted my first job as a news correspondent, I used to call Paris late every night with news from Czechoslovakia. The man on the other end of the wire took shorthand notes. There were actually two of them, and they took turns. I recognized them from their voices. Both were polite and always started with a *"Bon soir, monsieur,"* and ended by wishing me good night. After a while, I had the feeling that we knew each other and that a bond of friendship existed beween us, though we did not even know each other's names. I also did not know what my news partners looked like, whether they were young or middle-aged, whether they had a wife and children, where they lived, or other details. Physically we were very much separated. It was only a partial acquaintance or rather an incomplete one. But it was an acquaintance of some sort. News reporters have been making such acquaintances for decades.

There are still newer ways of getting acquainted resulting from technological inventions. I have in mind one widespread way—that of amateur radio broadcasters. They are also physically distant; they do not shake hands or know the face of their partners. But they have a special trait: They are not forced into acquaintance by sharing their office work or their newspaper reporting, but rather because of their interest in amateur broadcasting and their love for their hobby. Usually they are not anxious to meet. They want only to broadcast and receive news over the radio, and, since a broadcasting partner has to be a human, they have to accept him. Their inner motivation is not a concern for men but for machines. People are somehow only a forced addition. The partners are very distant; to a certain degree they can learn about each other, talk about their families, work, or worries, but usually they do not become intimate friends, for an interest in personal contact is lacking. The interest is only in broadcasting, and personal contact rarely takes place.

Forced acquaintance in the office or place of work is different. Here physical proximity can lead to personal interest or friendship. Many friendships develop in every place of work, sometimes even leading to marriage. I know of nothing of the sort among amateur broadcasters. Here partners are usually men, not people of both sexes, and distance is a serious obstacle.

In spite of distance, such acquaintances are valuable. One can receive news that does not appear in the newspapers, or additional details. I have the feeling of belonging to several faraway lands. The world becomes smaller, and a better understanding of morals and cultures begins to develop. And then, even if I do not have friends in foreign lands, I at least have acquaintances. And, if it happens that I visit a country where I have a radio partner, there would be someone I could visit, to whom I could turn. Thanks to another technical innovation—jet airliners—this happens more and more often.

In the history of mankind, this is an important step forward. It is one more way of getting acquainted, though certainly not the last one. In time a picture of the partner will be added to the voice. The facility of personal contact will increase.

People will be obligated to make acquaintance with a greater number of people. That will mean more contacts and more friends. But will these numerous friendships be as strong as the present ones? Will it mean more real bonds or just more polite, uninvolved relationships? It seems that man is not even capable of having many real friends. Emotionally he is not equipped for it, and perhaps it would not even give him pleasure. But he will certainly become more skillful in getting acquainted with an increasing number of people.

Actually we already have such people. They are politicians, for example. Their constant smiles, pats on the back and handshakes show something of the future man who will have to get acquainted with many people. Marconi did not know very well what the implications of his invention would be. He probably thought chiefly of the technical and not the human side. Besides, that's the case with other technical inventions as well.

Our Doors, Their Doors

I do not even know why I started talking about doors. I could have just as well talked about floors, furniture, or coffee mugs. I am thinking of all those household objects we see and touch daily and with which we have a certain personal, rather than merely utilitarian, relationship. We are used to such objects; we know how to handle them. Some, we are fond of; others irritate by their inappropriateness, elusiveness, ugliness, or what-have-you. Yes, we are esthetically, emotionally, personally, or otherwise attached to certain objects that surround us, or we are repelled by them. Of the Western World, only the Americans succeed in being personally disengaged from the objects of daily use. This is probably their strength and one of the reasons for their material success. Americans are not distracted or held back in their matter-of-fact judgments and decisions by this whole ballast of nonmaterialistic attitudes toward objects of daily use.

But we are different. I did not become fully aware of it until I became an exile in the United States. It also became clear to me why it is so hard for Americans to compose operas and some other forms of music: They lack these emotional attitudes toward objects and sometimes toward people. They don't know what to communicate with music or what to fill with it. But then Americans are more rational, especially in industry and commerce.

Well, then, in our rich attitude toward common objects,

there are some I would like to explore more fully. When we were living in Prague, all daily objects had, aside from the already mentioned qualities, an additional one which accompanied us in our daily life. It was the awareness that these were our own, Czech objects. Doors between rooms were of Czech wood, made by a Czech carpenter, varnished by a Czech worker, and inserted into the aperture between two rooms by a Czech carpenter. Even the door handles had been manufactured in our country. Not only that, the form and style of the doors and even the grease in the hinges were Czech. And so it was with other objects that surrounded us. The floors were made of our wood, cut in our sawmills, assembled by our workers, covered with our wax. There was a certain feeling of belonging, even of spiritual ownership. I do not mean legal ownership; the house with its doors, floors, windows, and walls belonged to the landlord. We were fully aware of it. But the furniture, cups, and plates belonged to us. Yet that was not the essential thing. What was important was that all those objects were of Czech origin, that they belonged to us through a higher law and that we felt at home among them just as we feel at home at mother's. It was a ubiquitous, irreplaceable bond, which made us feel really and fully at home.

In contrast to these, there were objects of foreign origin to which we could not develop any such attitude. For instance, in my bookcase, I also had French, English, and German books. But to us they were no more than guests. Even though we bought them, we did not own them in the same way as Czech books. Their authors lived somewhere else, went to schools other than the Czech ones, did not speak Czech, did not know our fields and meadows full of wild thyme, did not have Czech mothers or wives, did not eat roast goose with cabbage or liver sausages. The paper on which the books were printed was French, American, English, or German; the printing shop that printed them, the bookbinder that bound them and the thread he used, were foreign. It all had a certain charm, which also meant a certain distance. We liked these foreign guests, who made our lives more colorful; they were welcome, and we were glad that they had settled with us. So it was with other objects, such as a Daumier engraving, Swiss lace, or French perfume.

Then came exile. Do you realize how many bonds were torn? Not only with our loved ones, our town, our culture, our employment, but also those with objects of daily use. Were these bonds ever replaced by new ones? Or do we remain as in a vacuum? Neither one nor the other. We are surrounded by new objects. We live in a foreign house. We have one teaspoon from Czechoslovakia and how we value it! It is like a friend among strangers when I see it in the drawer among the other American teaspoons. It is like an old acquaintance we chance to meet at the movies or at a railway station. In spite of that, the other teaspoons are not foreigners. We have had them many years; we bought them; we own them—but somehow they are not completely ours. They were made in an American factory of American material and were given an American form.

And so it is with almost everything that surrounds us. We bought the house in which we live. But is it really ours? It has American windows, which do not open out but slide up; American door handles, which resemble big buttons; the house is of American wood and not of Czech bricks; and it has a cool cellar made of American cement. All the building material is American. If I touch the door, I feel it is their door and not our door; I feel that I am touching wood that did not grow in Czech forests, wood that is strange to me even if it serves as well as ours. Equally strange seem the floors, window frames, wooden stairs. The strangest of all seems to be the style in which the house is built. It was made neither by an architect nor a builder but by a carpenter. In our country, carpenters did not build houses. Every aspect of the house reminds me of the unknown American carpenter, a man probably simple, matter-of-fact, practical, but without any interest in style, or—better said—with an untrained, but essentially foreign style.

And so I live like a foreigner in my own house, among my own furniture, with my own objects. There are a few things which managed to give me a feeling of home in these strange surroundings. We have Czech books and an old picture of the Czech castle Hradčany. On the wall hangs a map of Bohemia, over three hundred years old, and an old plan of Prague from eighteenth century. My eyes touch these objects with feelings, touch the Czech teaspoon. They are a support to my Czech identity; they soothe my decimated feeling for home, and my soul, which will never again be young enough to create a new home in the full meaning of the word.

In spite of all this, "*panta rei*," as the Greeks used to say; everything is in motion. Even with the years, man still learns, though slowly and not too well. The wood on the doors of our house does not seem as strange as before, nor the wood of our furniture. Certainly I have no feeling of closeness or domesticity, but the feeling of strangeness grows duller. It is the result of my gradual adjustment to new surroundings. But there is something more to it. The more we hear news from Czechoslovakia of the moral and cultural decline, of the coarsening of daily life, of the decline of the Czech language and literature, the ignorance of Masaryk's ideals and the forgetting of Czech history, the more we feel that those things we valued are disappearing before our eyes. Much remains still, but it is mostly in ruins—tragic ruins, not ennobling or admirable ones. They are not like the ruins of the Romantics of the nineteenth century or the ruins that remained after the barbarian invasions. It is the work of vengeful destroyers of the Czech cultural heritage.

Ruins increase the desire for replacement; they support

our faster adjustment to a new home. But what a pity and what sorrow we feel! Is this a second exile or a culmination of the first?

A "Humanitarian" Spy

A spy always has an assumed identity; he cannot present himself as a spy; that is evident. And to a certain degree he really is the person he represents. The most common cover for a spy is to operate through a travel agency. This can be frequented by anyone, and such visits are inconspicuous. A spy can even come frequently, whenever he brings a message or expects one. His counterpart, the travel agent or the owner of the agency, also has an excellent cover. He occasionally conducts chartered trips abroad and thus meets his contacts unobtrusively.

During my life I have met several spies and very likely met some I did not recognize. Except for one, all of those I recognized were naïve. You could see through them easily, despite the fact that they carried out their tasks quite well. Even spies who are suspect can often perform their activities successfully. A person cannot very well have someone put in jail simply because he rightfully assumes that this person is a spy, the less so if it happens in a foreign land.

Such a situation confronted me when I came to the United States as a refugee. My first employment was at the University of Chicago. Quite by chance I got the same office that President Beneš had had during World War II. The moment I settled in my office, a student presented himself to me. He spoke in broken Slovak and introduced himself as the son of a Hungarian diplomat in the United States. He maintained that he was very fond of Slovaks and Czechs and that his fiancée was a Czech girl. He therefore came to see me so as to make the acquaintance of a Czech professor. He said it gave him pleasure. This was hard for me to believe; I was only too well aware of how the Hungarians dislike us. But perhaps there are exceptions, particularly among Hungarians with Czech fiancées.

The diplomat's son spent a little more than half an hour in my office. He asked me whether I had brought my family with me and whether my appointment to the University of Chicago was a permanent one. I said it was not and that I would be looking for another permanent appointment somewhere else. He wanted to know where. I answered that so far I had only one offer, from the University of Atlanta, but that I would wait to see whether I would receive others. Although he gave me an unpleasant feeling, I answered his questions, because job hunting was not an academic secret, let alone a political one. And indeed I told him just what he wanted to know and what the Czech Communists wanted to use against me. Shortly after, from a friend who reads Czech newspapers, I received a clipping from *Rudé Právo,* the Communist Party paper, about my current activities at the University of Chicago. It was typical Communist *"Dichtung und Wahrheit,"* a mixture of truth and lies, as Goethe called it. One point in it was especially interesting. The author of the article claimed that I would be sent to the University of Atlanta as an exponent of American Fascists and that I had been hired by the Ku Klux Klan to help oppress the Negroes. Such a *"Dichtung und Wahrheit"* would most assuredly have surprised even Goethe, just as it surprised me. Of course, Communists compose their fiction in a different way from Goethe. Even a small, trivial piece of information was good enough for constructing the great scandal.

Two other spies I have met were even more conspicuous. It was during the Prague uprising of 1945. At that time the

Czech National Council had just moved into the quarters of "Včela," on the Tyl Square, in Vinohrady. We had been in the building only a few hours when a blond "British parachutist" visited us, claiming that he was supposed to give news of the Prague uprising to the British army. He said he had two portable transmitters, and he was willing to give us one. We did not accept his offer, since we had a transmitter of our own. Moreover, in spite of his "British" uniform, he aroused our suspicion. How was it possible that his uniform was so neat and so well pressed? How was it possible that he could speak Czech so well? How did he know where the Czech National Council was located, when it was an absolute and recent secret? We should have had him taken into custody right away. But suppose he was really an Englishman, a member of the Allied army? We decided to let him go.

The moment he left, another man came, who claimed he was a Russian colonel, but whose uniform was of uncertain origin. When we found out that his Russian was very poor, he said that he was actually a Yugoslav in the services of the Soviet army. He offered us contact with the Red army. We rejected his offer too. He was in no hurry to leave and looked around attentively. He said he was not quite certain that we were the real Czech National Council, and evidently he wanted to learn as much as possible. What was decisive was that, soon after he left, German airplanes started bombing the building "Včela." The bombs did not score a hit, and we immediately moved to another place. As I see it, we had more good luck than good sense. Both visitors were probably German spies whom we should have immediately seized, but we were green, and then there were those Allied uniforms! Our luck outweighed our naïveté.

All three spies were striking and invited suspicion. In spite of their conspicuousness, they carried out their mission successfully. Now I would like to mention a very inconspicuous spy, whom I never suspected. He claimed to be a Polish newspaperman in Prague. I made his acquaintance shortly after the Ministry of Education (following the suggestions of Dr. Rouček and myself) created the School of Political and Social Sciences. Dr. Rouček became rector, and I was chosen dean of the Political Faculty. One night, at about eleven-fifteen, Dr. Rouček telephoned to say that a certain Mr. Stankiewicz, a Polish correspondent, would very much like to make my acquaintance. He was said to have heard many nice things about my political and scientific achievements. I was told that he and the correspondent were sitting in a wine cellar in Malá Strana and that they would very much like me to join them there. Even though Dr. Rouček and I were good friends, I did not accept the invitation because I would have returned home very late. Maybe some other time.

When we met shortly afterwards in the same wine cellar, Mr. Stankiewicz made a very good impression on me. He was rather young and had a lot of youthful enthusiam. After a while he asked me to take a walk with him outside in the glow of the setting sun. Slowly and quite inconspicuously he started talking about his humanitarian ideals, to which he was completely dedicated. He saw his journalistic profession as serving those ideals. We must strive to achieve good will among nations and lasting, permanent peace. He said he was quite active in this respect and therefore had taken the liberty of asking me to meet him. People who think alike must make each other's acquaintance and reinforce each other. Perhaps we would be able to cooperate on some project. Mr. Stankiewicz was also religious, and his belief in God and his humanitarian ideals were intertwined. His belief was not that of organized religion. God exists for all people and for members of all churches. In spite of his timid enthusiasm, Mr. Stankiewicz was not pitiful. He presented me his opinions quietly, almost shyly. His humanitarianism affected me. We shook hands like two people who understand each other and returned to the wine cellar. I met Mr. Stankiewicz a few more times. He even visited us with his wife. He never pried into my affairs, he never asked direct questions, but he certainly must have learned a lot from our discussions of various political problems. He judged everything from the standpoint of his deep humanitarian convictions. He seemed well educated and intelligent. Perhaps, had his knowledge of the Czech language been better, I would have been more suspicious, but his awkward use of Czech expressions seemed to be a sufficient explanation for any nascent doubts that might otherwise have developed in my mind.

When toward the end of 1947 I was supposed to make an official visit to the United States, I considered taking the Polish ship *Batory*, but Mr. Stankiewicz strongly warned me against it. He said it was dangerous and that I could be arrested in Poland. His warning increased my confidence in his sincerity. Then came the Communist coup and exile. Soon after, while in a refugee camp in Germany, I received a letter from Mr. Stankiewicz. He had left for Germany before the coup, apparently on a journalistic assignment. He wrote that it was dangerous for him to continue working in Czechoslovakia. He wanted to know how I was and what the conditions were in the camp. I sent him a fairly long reply because I had plenty of time. We exchanged several more letters. All of a sudden Mr. Stankiewicz fell silent. After some time the *Stars and Stripes* published the news that he had been arrested and sentenced to ten years as a Communist spy. Besides other material in his possession were found several letters from a political and scholarly personality who was at the time living in a camp in Germany.

Everything became clear, but Mr. Stankiewicz came to my mind often nevertheless. Surely he had spied on several fronts. He certainly was not devoted to humanitarian ideals, as he pretended. He probably played this role only in front of me. Among his victims I was probably the only one who was impressed by his humanitarian ideals. He had probably created a special identity only for me. He certainly showed different faces to other people. How many faces did he have? And how was it possible that he, a cynical man, could have pretended to be a humanitarian so convincingly? Was he equally successful in adopting other convictions and personalities? He was probably a talented man, perhaps more gifted than most spies. He was also better educated. And he was probably the only spy who fooled one of his victims by assuming humanitarian ideals. It must have given him a lot of work. He was a very diligent and original spy. How different Mr. Stankiewicz was from the types of spies we know from movies and detective novels! Yes, life is sometimes richer than an artist's fantasy, and it was my fate to be the object of this unique method.

American Generosity

When I think of the case of Mrs. Blake, I am tempted to say "American goodness of heart." Yet, I hesitate to apply the term "goodness" to all Americans. They are hardhearted in business and toward their subordinates. They are definitely not openhearted, nor, as we used to say, smooth of manner. But they are definitely generous. American higher education and charitable institutions are for the most part supported by donations from private and corporate gifts and legacies. A hard American businessman considers it his duty to give a certain amount of money yearly to some good cause. But is he openhearted in our sense of the word? Does he contribute to good causes out of the goodness of his heart or because he is led by Christian ideals? Is he magnanimous in some matters and a hard businessman in others? Does he have a split personality? And what about Mrs. Blake? Was she an openhearted woman or was she merely generous? Was she an honest Christian who gave her tithes? Perhaps she should be characterized in still other ways. I cannot say because I did not know her personally. I never met her; we just corresponded for a short time.

This correspondence was initiated in an unusual way. I had received a letter from a former student of mine at Charles University. At the time of writing he was about thirty-five years old. He wrote that he would like to finish his studies at our university. He asked for my help because admission to

87

our university was quite difficult. I promised to do whatever I could.

When he arrived, he brought along a host of documents from Charles University, which facilitated matters considerably. It also helped that I could present him with good conscience as a talented and enterprising man, for I had known this side of him from his outstanding work in student groups. He was so energetic that, in student matters, he often personally successfully contacted members of the government.

Mr. Nechleba was therefore a promising young man, and I could support his application and his transfer of the highest possible credits. I obtained more for him than I had expected. But to study at an American university one needs money, and Mr. Nechleba had none. He did have a supporter, Mrs. Blake from Chicago; she would send him enough to cover tuition and expenses. Yet shortly afterwards it was I who received the money from her. In a letter she asked me to pay for what he needed and then to give him pocket money, ten dollars at a time. She wrote that he did not know how to handle money.

It was all very strange to me; after all, Mr. Nechleba was a grown man. But in two days I understood. Mr. Nechleba bought a hundred-and-eighty-dollar camera on credit. Although he did not know them, he gave a dinner, complete with wine and cognac, for the president and the dean of the university. He also invited a professor he had just met, the businessman from whom he had bought the camera, several students, and me. It all cost a lot of money. He also had a telephone installed and immediately made several long distance calls. He wanted me to pay for all this out of the money Mrs. Blake had sent. Why didn't I write her; she would certainly send more money. I ended up by thanking her for the amount I had received and cautioning her that Mr. Nechleba had run up more debts. By return mail she sent more money, which I doled out in small amounts. I wondered how I had been chosen for this function and why Mrs. Blake trusted me. I also would have liked to know why Mrs. Blake gave money to Mr. Nechleba at all. I assumed that she must be very rich.

Mr. Nechleba eventually explained everything. Mrs. Blake was not rich; she worked as a secretary in a big business firm in which her husband was a minor clerk. They had no children. And how could a Czech student have made her acquaintance? Just by chance, in a bus. It was a cold winter day, and he had had no overcoat. They had sat next to each other and struck up a conversation. He said that he was a refugee and that he would like to continue his studies in the United States. He confessed he had neither job nor money. Mrs. Blake offered to buy him an overcoat; Mr. Nechleba accepted after the appropriate surprise and deliberation. She bought him a beautifully fitted, expensive overcoat, and also offered him a small sum of money. She said that they would have to talk some more, and invited him to her apartment. Her husband took a liking to him, and the upshot of the visit was that the Blakes offered to support Mr. Nechleba in his studies. Mr. Nechleba did not hesitate to accept. The Blakes gave him money for his trip to our university town and added pocket money in return for his promise to let them know how much he would need for tuition, room and board, and so forth. From their brief contacts in Chicago, the Blakes had learned that Mr. Nechleba could not handle money. So they asked for more details about me as his former and future professor and got my address.

Then followed what I have already described. I received money from Mrs. Blake periodically and willy-nilly became Mr. Nechleba's guardian and treasurer. My efforts, of course, led nowhere, because he spent money at a fantastic rate. But the spree did not last long; Mr. Nechleba fell ill and stopped studying. All his debts were paid by Mrs. Blake (through me), except for the large telephone bill. The Bell Telephone Company did not know of Mrs. Blake's existence, nor of her willingness to pay his debts. Mr. Nechleba disappeared without leaving a forwarding address.

The case shook me a little. How different the Americans are from us! I recalled all the innumerable presents to universities, often from individuals of limited means, all the donations to charitable organizations, all the support for research into polio, cancer, and such. It seemed to me that I now understood Americans better. And what about the Marshall Plan? Was it only a means to stop the spread of Communism in Europe or was it also part of the cultural heritage of generosity toward the needy? Was it not an endeavor to help someone who was trying hard to lift himself by his bootstraps? Was not Mr. Nechleba Mrs. Blake's little "Marshall Plan"? And did he not turn out like the underdeveloped nation that recklessly spends money on magnificent buildings, airplanes, sumptuous uniforms for generals, and luxury for its UN representatives, a nation with which the United States has infinite patience in the hopes that it will finally find the right way? Yes, Americans are not only generous; they are also patient.

And yet Mrs. Blake had one trait I cannot find in the Marshall Plan or other charitable actions. Every year she sends me a Christmas greeting. Why? Does she add a little bit of heart to the prevailingly rational cultural trait of generosity? Or is it just politeness toward someone who had helped her in her little Marshall Plan? I do not know, but the Christmas greeting always pleases me and stirs something in me. I say "something" because I still do not fully understand American generosity.

An Envelope

Envelopes for letters are a fairly modern device. In former times letters were simply folded, sealed and the address was written on the outside; therefore the address remained on the back side of the letter even after it was opened. This had a certain advantage; it gave the name and address of the addressee. Today we rarely have this information in a personal letter; the only clear indication of the addressee is usually his first name. If a letter begins "Dear friend," or something similar, it gives no visible sign as to whom it was addressed. And this is a pity. We simply have to guess from the handwriting, from the signature, which again may be only a first name, to whom and by whom the letter was written.

I have in my possession the original of an old letter. It was written by the French King Henry IV to a Captain de Dussac four hundred years ago. Yet, despite its age, it remains easily identified; as usual in those days, it has the address on the back.

We are no longer able to do this. We open a letter and throw the envelope in the wastebasket. Often we even tear it up. I once knew a man who always carefully opened the envelope, read the letter, put it back in the envelope, and then filed it. That's how he saved letters for some seventy years. He was my great uncle, a tenant of a large estate, who died at the age of ninety. After his death, my great aunt asked me to go through his correspondence. It was not particularly interesting. For me, a college student, the only things of interest were the postage stamps, some of which were very old, but I noted, too, how nice it is to know the name of the addressee and of the sender. Already the form of the old envelopes, the color of the paper, the postmark, and the stamp itself made the letters a historical document, evidence of a certain era.

Today we remove this patina from the letters as we neglect the identity of the addressee. We take away certain important characteristics from the letter and actually preserve only its body. Envelopes serve their purpose by helping the letter get delivered. It is a short-term service, and having fulfilled that task they become litter, objects, which for a time increase the disorder on our desk and get thrown away as soon as possible.

About two years ago I made an exception. I took an envelope that, contrary to my habit, I did not tear up or throw away, but used as a coaster on the nightstand on which I put a glass of water every evening to quench my thirst during the night. This is typical of an exile. Back home I would not have done it. I would get a real coaster, as would be fitting for an orderly man, but as exiles we develop many unusual habits. Nor have we any desire to get rid of them, knowing we are not really at home. I am, after all, only an exile.

The older this envelope grows, the more interesting it becomes. Being more and more careful not to spill water on it, I am in some way fully aware that I am trying to prolong its life, and that as long as possible. Since I have had it for two years, why couldn't I have it five, or perhaps even more? It surprises me by its still good shape, and it seems to me that with proper handling it could last a long time. Then after many years I shall look at it, read in the upper left-hand corner who sent it to me, and say, "Look, this was sent to me by my former student at Charles University (or perhaps a former member of parliament, or someone else)." It is part of my game with the envelope that I do not look at what is written on it. This is deliberate, but I do not even know why I do it. Whenever I put a glass of water on it, I am always pleased that I have prolonged its life for one more day. And, as I said, I shall continue doing it for a long time. There is something odd in this act of mine. Before going to bed I usually think: Such a trivial thing, yet it is still here, it still serves me.

It's a kind of a game. When I see the envelope in the evening I realize how transitory it is, made of fragile material, which I should have disposed of like any reasonable person. But it pleases me to protect its fragility, to overcome the flimsiness of its material and prolong its usefulness for years. Just like that! To add a few years of service. And in order to make it possible, I had to transfer it from one function to another, like a clerk or soldier who is transferred from one post to another. Yes, to an object whose use was temporary I accorded a new, more permanent usefulness, which it can keep for many years. It is like giving an assistant clerk, whose duties were temporary, the new duties of a clerk with tenure. My envelope received such a tenure from me. Tenure, of course, is nothing permanent; a person leaves to retire or to die. And so it will be with my envelope. One day its usefulness will end, and it will end up in the wastebasket.

I am aware that I am playing a strange, perhaps childish game with my envelope. Perhaps no one else plays such games. I have the feeling I should stop it. Yet, on the other hand, I think: Is it not good that I can still play, that something remains in me from the time when play was expected of me? And, if it pleases me, why give it up? Nobody even knows about it. It cannot harm me either in my work or in contact with other people. And it makes my life a little more colorful, so why not?

Unpaid Debts

Many people have debts not only to banks but also to friends and acquaintances. I also have debts, and I feel them keenly, certainly more than other debtors. They are not monetary debts, which I have always carefully avoided, but moral ones. And those can weigh on the mind more than the others.

I felt this obligation toward a man who was very dear to me during his lifetime. After his death, I feel this debt even more, because I cannot repay him or his survivors. In this respect, moral debts are worse than monetary ones. The latter we can repay to the estate, the former we cannot. As a rule, for the estate they have only an insignificant meaning or none at all.

Of course, there are degrees of moral debt. If someone has rendered us a great service by giving us a job or saving our life, after his death we can render service to his children or his widow. But not all moral debts are of this type. Sometimes there are no survivors, or the survivors are not in need of anything. Sometimes—and this my unfortunate case—the debt can be paid only to the benefactor.

For about sixteen years I knew a physician who was an exile like me. Soon I became his patient. He was a German Jew from the vicinity of Pilsen, but he could speak Czech very well. This was great comfort to me in my many illnesses. When a person does not feel well, it is a great relief to talk about it in his own tongue; in foreign surroundings the mother tongue becomes part of the healing process.

Moreover, this physician was an extremely kind, goodnatured man, not like some of our Czech doctors, jovial and gruff. He always invited patients into his consulting room with a warm smile and a friendly nod of his head. They felt a little better even before entering his office. And this kindly and encouraging attitude prevailed throughout the examination, the writing of the prescription and the advice on how to combat the illness. He had a genuine, deeply human interest in his patients, and, whenever possible, he did for them more than was his mere medical duty. He thought through for them what they might do in their situation, and accompanied all with a warm, sincere smile. He devoted himself to them from morning till night. One can say that he sacrificed his life to his patients.

When I think of him and visualize his whole life filled with service to the ill, I see him as a Jewish saint. It is a contradiction, for Jews do not have saints. But it is still the most fitting expression for this extraordinarily kind man.

Even though this term never crossed my mind during his lifetime, I was clearly aware that he was morally and humanly extraordinary. And it is a well-known fate of saints to be recognized for the most part after their death. I made the decision to give my Jewish saint full recognition during his lifetime. I felt that I had to tell him that he was the kindest man I have ever known. It would be the least that he deserved. Those long years of thoughtfulness, service and good cheer deserved much more. But I never gave him even this small token. I was always about to do it whenever I had an appointment with him. Of course, during the examination there was no time for it, and it was somehow not fitting. But there were other occasions. When he fell ill, I used to visit him with my wife. But his wife was always present, and in this company of four I hesitated to say what was on my mind. Of course, my smile and expression gave some testimony to him of my relation to him. Yet I constantly felt that I should express my appreciation more explicitly. When he suddenly lost consciousness, I lost my last chance. Maybe his dying would have been made a little easier, had he known what I thought of him and how much I appreciated him. It would have been a small repayment for all his goodness. And I did not give this to him. I will always remain his debtor. It is a debt that cannot be repaid, and that will trouble me a long time.

Unfortunately it is not my only debt to this dear man. Through my carelessness I added another one. During our next to last visit with him I mentioned that we were going to visit our son Pavel and his wife to meet our new granddaughter. The good doctor sent our son his most sincere greetings. While he was aware that he would soon die, he thought of other people and wanted to show some kindness to them. And he knew my son only distantly. I related his good wishes to Pavel and reminded him that these were precious greetings from a man who knew that he would soon die. My son appreciated it and asked me to return the good wishes most cordially. Unfortunately I never gave him these greetings. I reproach myself with it, even though it was not altogether my fault. Our good doctor suddenly felt better, could easily walk around the room, and after a long time was again able to laugh. We all thought it was a real turn for the better. In reality, it was the respite that sometimes precedes death. No one suspected it. We saw each other for the last time in a very gay mood and in high spirits. It never occurred to me to relay my son's greetings to him. Everything seemed to recede into the background in view of this sudden and joyful turn for the better. We parted with the feeling that we would certainly see each other soon. In reality we parted forever.

No one knows about my debts. They are not a blemish on my character. Nobody will ever ask me to repay them. But they feel heavy, maybe just because they can never be repaid.

Conversations with the Deceased

The older I grow and the more my friends depart, the more I find myself talking with some of them in my mind. It is not in a dream. During the day, whenever I remember one of them, I might say, "Look, I am already a grandfather!" Or, "What is your opinion about the changes in the USSR?" or, "How would you deal with the problems I am having just now?" But the fact that I need their advice is not the most important part of our conversations. This probably happens to many people. What is more important is that I almost always "talk" with people who were older than I and who represented authority to me, at least in some respect. I esteemed them because they were older, and more experienced, and also because of their position. There was between us a difference of age and of judgment, maturity, and perspective.

I turn with great pleasure to these older and esteemed friends, wishing that my relationship with them could be as before. But it is not possible. They stopped while I went on. How good it would be if they could have gone on with me up to this day, or if our relationship could have been fixed as it was before their death! We understood each other so well and I was so used to them; they were part of my world, a world to which I was adjusted, one which was comforting to me, and in which I made my plans and acted.

Unfortunately, the more the years since their death pass, the more I lose ground under my feet, and the more I feel I am alone. My conversations with the dead have gaps, which are getting larger. It is not that the lapse of time diminishes my esteem and respect. It is not because they have changed (that is, after all, not possible), or because my attitude toward them has changed. It is nothing of the sort. But there are other changes: every year I grow older. And in ten years that makes quite a difference.

Take my father, for instance. I was thirty-two years his junior. This difference between us always remained the same, even when he grew older and I grew more mature. I have always talked to him as to an elder, and I showed respect toward his age, experiences, and outlook. And so it is still in my conversations with him. But into this stable and warm relationship penetrate more and more disturbing elements. For instance, I tell my father in a nice way what I intend to do. He nods his head and smiles. Occasionally he shows pleasure about this or that part of my conversation; occasionally he looks at me with understanding, and sometimes he says, "You know, at this point I would be careful. Something could happen." And I accept it with seriousness and respect: "I think you are right, Tati. Here I must proceed more cautiously." And then again I continue my conversation as if nothing had happened. He listens carefully and with interest, smiling at me in a fatherly way. He is still father to me, as he used to be. It is so nice and cordial! But it does not last long, it cannot last long. Suddenly I tell my father, "Tati, do you know that now I am only ten years younger than you?" By that I mean ten years younger than he was when he died. "And soon I shall be as old as you were."

It is a rather strange feeling to see one's father as nearly as old or about to be fully as old as oneself. Maybe someday, if I live that long, I shall be able to say: "Tati, I am now older than you were. Actually we are now peers. I am probably more experienced and maybe even wiser through my accumulated

98

experiences. You do not even know that Germany lost the war, that I took part in the Prague uprising, that I became full professor at Charles University, that I held a prominent political office, and that Communist terror overtook our country."

Of course, I shall never tell this to my father even in my mind. In my conversations with him I shall always keep the attitude of a son. I cannot possibly look at him as someone younger than I. I shall never be able to tell him: "Tati, you cannot be so well informed; you are younger than I!" He will always be a father to me; I shall always have filial respect for him; I shall always take him for older and more experienced, even if this bears no relation to reality. Reality is weaker and less convincing than my filial respect. Personal relationships and their peculiar nature are stronger than facts. And this is good. At least it makes my life easier.

My conversations are not, of course, limited to the people nearest to me. But they are always with people who had meant something to me or had influenced me. For instance, I sometimes talk with the former minister of our political party, Dr. Ripka. He was five years my senior and unusually intelligent; we shared an interest in foreign affairs, in hunting (sometimes we went hunting together); we were both members of our party. I greatly valued his political opinions; for me he was an authority. He remained so in exile, where we cooperated on the Council for a Free Czechoslovakia. During the meetings of the council, his opinions had a ring of authority for me, even if I did not agree with him. And now I am five years older than he was. In my conversations with the dead, I could tell him: "Look, brother, now I am five years older than you and have so many more experiences than you. You did not live through Stalin's downfall from his heavenly pedestal, you did not witness the removal of his body from Lenin's Tomb, or even the destruction of his huge statue in Prague; you did not witness the rupture between China and Russia, the flights

99

into space, the seeming liberalization of Communism in Russia and in our country, the flight of Stalin's daughter to the United States, and many other things that would have interested you. I know so much more than you could have known!" But I never talk in my mind with him in this way. I still have the same relationship with him as before. In his keen and wise opinions, I always see something authoritative that I respect, even though he is so much poorer than I in political experiences.

I have the same trouble with his age as with my father's. When we converse, I am not certain whether he remains older or has become younger than I. When we begin, he is always older. My attitude of respect and esteem for my elder will always remain with me. But when we talk about concrete political problems, there is always something of what he never lived through, of what he missed by his untimely death that reminds me that he is actually that much younger than I.

When a composition by Bohuslav Martinû is presented at our university, I often imagine him listening and being content, or perhaps dissatisfied, with the performance. I see him in front of me in his student days when he sometimes visited our family. He was a young, unknown composer. Nobody called him "maestro," only "*M. Martinû.*" He was a violinist with the Czech Philharmonic Orchestra, and had completed his studies in Paris with the composer Roussel. For me, he was an authority on music. And now, when I talk to him, I am much older than the young man who stood smiling by our piano and listened to the French pianist Marcelle Bousquet perform his compositions. Most often I ask this young man how he likes it that his compositions are performed all over the world and that, a long time after his death, his compositions talk to me from the podium of an American university. Other times I ask him what he thinks of contemporary electronic music. But he did not live to know it and cannot tell me anything about it.

Yes, we have difficulties with our dead. They remain part of our world but recede from it bit by bit. They are an essential part of our lives, but they gradually lose their essence. Nevertheless, they retain an important position in our spiritual life. For many years, we have that difficult, dual attitude toward them. And then, if we live long enough, we solve this dilemma by relegating them to history with the understanding that they have only a historical connection with our world. They may be part of the history of our family or of our political party or nation, as were, for instance, our important journalist Havlíček or our famous historian, Palacký. Even if I had known them personally, I probably would not ask them what would be best to do in this or that situation. And I might not even ask such an authority as our first president, Thomas G. Masaryk. Only in the most intimate and personal matters can our nearest ones remain our advisors, capable of conversation with us. I shall always be able to tell my mother that I shall soon retire, that our children are grown, or perhaps that I often have a backache or do not go hunting anymore, and other such things.

Not only does the world of the living change; so does that of the dead. All our lives we have to nurture some ability to adjust. And new adjustment is always difficult. Of course, it is a part of life, and a part of the life lived in relation to those who can no longer change, because they live no longer.

A Traitor among Us

The mere likelihood that we might harbor a traitor among us is horribly upsetting. It creates unfounded suspicion of innocent people; it strains ties of friendship; it destroys the institution in which we work or the circle of friends to which we belong. Those who are innocent try to detect the real traitor and eliminate the suspicion that strains them and the other innocent people in their group. It is necessary to resolve the situation radically, to clear the air so as to live and work normally; it is necessary to rid the family, the work group, or even the nation of a paralyzing tension and suspicion that interferes with human relations.

Yes, with an unknown traitor it is hard to live, but it is harder still to live with a traitor we know. Every society destroys traitors as fast and as energetically as possible. We had several such experiences during the war and after. But they were comparatively rare. We knew people who reported to the German occupiers and others who later reported to the Communists. Only for the sake of extreme caution did we sometimes wait to deal with them. In the meantime they were isolated; they were not given access to information; they were quietly shunted to a siding. That is the least one can do to a traitor when one cannot deal with him in a more radical way. When it is possible, then we do not hesitate. The reaction toward a traitor is usually rapid and resolute, even if it is sometimes quiet and outwardly inconspicuous. No society wants to live with a traitor, to allow him to take part in its life, to have him for a member.

So I was nettled by the idea that in exceptional circumstances it does not necessarily have to be this way, but only in those where the traitor cannot betray anymore, when he actually is not a whole man anymore. Maybe you ask what I mean by that? How someone can be less than a whole man? I will explain it more fully.

During World War II a young, handsome teacher taught in a small town. I did not know him personally; I had only heard about him. He was an opportunist, who wanted to build a quick career. He believed that Germany would win the war and bet all his cards on its victory. He collaborated fully and openly for several years, causing tremendous offense and disgust. People shunned him. He took it hard, but there was no going back. Besides, the expectation of a final German victory and an excellent career fortified and sustained him.

Then came the victory of the Allies and with it the complete shattering of all his dreams. The strong and radical reaction, by which people of all groups excise and punish, had to come; he was prosecuted, sentenced to death, and executed. He was one of the very small number of Czechs who were punished in this way. But this teacher-traitor had his value even after his execution. Physicians noticed that his body was unusually well formed, and the professor of anatomy asked the authorities to give his skeleton to the institute of anatomy.

The body of the traitor was immersed in a strong acid solution, which dissolved the soft parts of the body. Only the skeleton remained, and today, after more than twenty years, it serves medical students in their studies of anatomy. Since human bones are extremely durable (some are even millions of years old), it will serve medical students even in the next generation and ones to follow. For generations, the traitor will be among our young people; the hands of medical students

will touch his bones, study their shape and functional inter-
dependence, move his limbs. The traitor's skeleton will answer
their questions patiently, for many decades, and always truthfully and correctly. Will this be a lengthy purgatory, will it
atone for sins committed during the traitor's life? To a certain
extent, perhaps. It will definitely be of some service to the
nation he betrayed. It is a service that he did not choose, and
that he renders only involuntarily. But it is undoubtedly a
valuable service.

That teacher-traitor was actually sentenced twice: first, to
lose his life, and second, to atone for his guilt by serving in
the anatomical institute. While he could not be thankful for
the first verdict, he could have been grateful for the second,
provided something Czech remained in him. And, I believe,
this might have been true.

And now what is life like with such a traitor after his
execution, or rather with his skeleton? At first the students,
assistants, and professors were aware of his guilt. They considered his guilt as expiated and did not show him any hate. He
became a tolerated member of the medical group, a quiet and
passive member. He answered the students' questions, gave
them needed information, was of service in their studies, and,
through them, also served future physicians' patients. The
students debated the various qualities of the bones, formed
common opinions and ideas. All these were activities of the
living, but he was an essential part of them. He was at the
center of an exchange of ideas and the formation of common
opinions. He was like someone who keeps quiet while everyone
is talking. Yet his reticence means something and has an influence on the ideas and feelings of people who converse. Their
ideas and maybe even feelings might be different if he were
not present. Even ideas of medical students in the presence of
a skeleton are different from those when the skeleton is not
there. It seems to me that his participation in the medical

students' life is not much different from that of ancestral masks in religious ceremonies of patrician families of ancient Rome. Their actual activity had probably been long forgotten, their ideas and opinions were not known anymore, and yet they influenced the living at least by being considered legal members of the family and by their masks being physically present. Our traitor influenced with his skeleton. It was, at least partly, the material remains of his former personality. Of the ancestors of the Roman families, nothing physical remained. Their masks were only substitutes. Of course, the skeleton at the anatomical institute does not have family ties with anyone of those with whom it is in contact. But it does belong to another institution of which the medical students are members—to the anatomical institute and to a living group of the young people who use it in their studies, who talk about it, and who, with its help, prepare for their future.

His usefulness in the lives of medical students, of course, did not cease with the succeeding generation. Nothing was known anymore about the guilt of this unfortunate man. And yet, he remained active in a peculiar way in the lives of the living people. The dead have so many ways of influencing the living: Authors, composers, painters, philosophers, religious thinkers of former times—all remain a living part of present-day life. Of course, that is because they contributed something valuable, because they helped with the development of our culture. This teacher-traitor still affects the living—not because he contributed something during his life; just the opposite, because he worked against the values and interests of a nation and its cultural life. This negative activity brought him to the gallows and into the anatomical institute. Usually the institute receives the remains of poor people who have neither achieved anything great nor done anything unlawful. But he, a lonely exception, drew my attention.

A Hesitating Drop of Water and Other Thoughts

I know that it is a title that will tell the reader very little. Instead of indicating what he will encounter, it expects him to read at least part of the story to understand it. But why can't things be turned upside down, against normal expectations, especially as it will not result in an international incident?

I should say right off (though it shouldn't be so, since my topic is hesitating drops) that I have never systematically observed drops of water and their travels down windowpanes. But I have given them some of my marginal, unsystematic attention. Usually I was thinking of something else and then noticed, on the margin of my attention, that a certain drop of water on my study's windowpane suddenly started moving. It was during a rainstorm or shortly thereafter. In the kitchen, where there is a lot of steam from cooking, a drop often stops for a while, as if the steam were hindering its movement. But raindrops, too, stop on their way and later continue. I always have the feeling that they have exhausted their energy and await a recharge from new raindrops. Often I understood (especially in the case of drops inside the kitchen windows), that they lost some weight on their way down and for a while were too light to continue. Later on, vapor adds to their weight and the drops continue on their way.

On a larger windowpane, this can be repeated several

times. The drop is like a traveler to a faraway land who stops several times to verify his route; he makes sure and proceeds to his destination. The destination for a drop of water is always the bottom rim of the frame where the drop dissolves into the water that accumulated from previous drops; for the drop, it is the end of its individual existence, while for the traveler it need not be so.

Maybe the reader who has had enough instruction in physics is smiling and thinking that I fail to understand the travel of drops. And he may be right. But I would like to continue my reflections about drops just the same, if only because it interests me.

In the drop running down the windowpane I see something alive, almost human. It seems to me that the drop wants to come down, that it meets obstacles in its way, that it ponders how to overcome them, arrives at a certain decision and starts on its way until a new obstacle comes along. It is, of course, a very old custom and sometimes a necessity for people to anthropomorphize material things or animals. It is unscientific and should not be done. Educated people try to resist it, but do not succeed. Sometimes it is not even possible. Or, it is possible but not worth the trouble, since it makes our conception of the world less human. Somehow we do not like a dehumanized world.

Let's look again at the drop. Can one identify with a raindrop, with its purely physical nature? It is actually not possible. We can watch it; we can look for the laws of its movements, as, for instance, a physicist would do, but that is all. We cannot "think" or "feel" as it does, for a raindrop neither thinks nor feels. It does not even "behave" in the same sense that animals and sometimes people behave (I have in mind the behavioral sciences). It observes certain laws of nature, but knows nothing about them. Isn't that conception empty? Don't we have to add something to make the world around us more human? It seems to me that we almost have to.

If I see lightning and hear thunder, I have the feeling that someone up there wanted to give vent to his enormous energy. It is as if someone were saying: "Now I've shown them, but at the same time I did not want to harm anyone." My thinking is not "wise," but I cannot help it and I must say I do not even want to do otherwise. If I come to a flooded river, I feel something terribly heedless, moving, something that says: "Everyone, get out of my way! I spare no one, I don't fool around. Take that into consideration and act accordingly!" I feel that even the muddy water points to bad character. But when I watch a landslide or an avalanche, no such thoughts come to my mind. I rather think that both forces have feelings of guilt, as if they said, "Excuse me for having slid so clumsily, I could not hold it too well. I did not want to do anything of the sort, but I could not help it."

Perhaps, looking at a grand piano, everyone feels that its legs are carrying a great weight, that they are expending a lot of energy and that their work never ends—except possibly, when the piano is no longer used. It has been said for a long time that church spires seem to point to heaven, although in reality they do nothing of the sort. They are just motionless, lifeless stones, which we bring to life.

Even in cases where similarity is considerable, our minds make it even greater. I might, for instance, fall off a rock, bounce several times, and finally hit bottom. Later I might observe the fall of a boulder and on the basis of my experience empathize with it completely. While this "feeling" does not reflect reality, I feel subjective in that I understand the fall of the boulder better.

I should stay with the drop of water or other animated lifeless things, but I am tempted to tackle living things, which, though alive already, we enliven further with feelings and thoughts. We make them into beings we can understand. For us, what is actually going on inside them is not enough; we have to supplement reality, often at the price of arranging it and leaving out facts inconvenient to our conception.

On the other hand, the error is lesser, since something does actually happen inside the animals. They may be hungry or angry or showing devotion to their masters. We do not have to put such feelings into them. Of course, their thoughts are much less clear than ours, if it can be said that they have thoughts at all. If they do not (which is most often the case), we add them ourselves and then understand our animals more fully.

When our cat approaches a dish of freshly cut liver, he goes slowly, with dignity, as if he wanted to show that he is not greedy, voracious, or materialistically inclined. He certainly has no ideas of the sort. He does not even attempt to act dignified, as it appears to us. It is part of his behavior, but we like to see something more in it, something human. When he comes to the dish, he stops, lifts his head a little, and then lowers it. He repeats this several times, as if he wanted to say, "Well, well, let's see what we have here today." If he likes it, he comes closer and sniffs the liver thoroughly. It seems as if he said to himself, "I have to make certain that it is fresh; otherwise I will not eat it. I do not have to eat everything, I am not that hungry." And, if in his opinion it is not suitable, he turns around and goes away. This departure may be definitive or only temporary. He can wait nearby, his back turned away from the food he had refused, and "think" as if he said, "Well, it is not too good, but I could try it. I shall see; I can always stop." Then he returns and usually eats some of it.

How many ideas I have imputed to the mind of our cat! And all of them are human. Very likely none of them went through his head. He simply recognized the food, which is probably automatic, partly inborn, and partly the result of experience. Neither rejecting the food, leaving the scene, nor waiting and returning are connected with the thoughts that I so willingly attribute to the small brain of our cat. I imagine that the cat's behavior is the result of two opposite forces. One is hunger (an inborn instinct), the other (also instinctive) is a dislike for meat that is not quite fresh. And our meat is never really fresh. We get it in a supermarket several days after the animals have been slaughtered. Even if it is frozen and well preserved, it never tastes quite fresh. The big cats kill and devour on the spot as much meat as their stomachs will hold. The ancestors of our pet cats treated smaller animals the same way.

And now tell me whether we prefer the cat to whom we ascribe human qualities or the cat which is probably torn by conflict between instincts?

It is clear that the thoughts we ascribe to a cat make him much closer to us. We like him because we think he resembles us. We also possess both of those instincts. But they are, surprisingly, less attractive to us than thoughts and feelings, even if they are only imagined.

It seems that we personify the world to feel more at home in it, to like it more. And can anyone wonder at us, since there are so many things to like? We would rather live with joy than without.

A List of the Deceased

A list of the deceased. Who makes one for himself? I do not know anyone who does. Of course, some institutions make lists of deceased for practical reasons. There are financial claims of survivors. Some communities make lists of fallen soldiers, to honor them with a monument on which their names are inscribed. But individuals like me do nothing of the sort. There was one well-known literary character, so truthfully described by Gogol, who made a list of deceased peasants from large estates that did not belong to him. To appear to society as a rich man, he needed a great number of names. So he made a list of the dead, who, however, played the role of the living. For personal reasons, the impostor created the institution of a "rich firstborn son." He was an exception even among impostors.

Yet, last night, I discovered that I, too, have been making a list of the deceased without being aware of it. And, without doubt, it is written by my own hand. The first idea that will probably occur to you is that I am peculiar. In reality I am not, at least I think not.

I discovered the existence of the list by chance when I looked into my address book to find the most recent address of an acquaintance I wanted to write to. I came across the name of another acquaintance, who had died this year. And soon I found a second and a third one. Then I stopped looking for the address of the man to whom I wanted to write and who (very likely) was still among the living. I looked only for the names of the deceased, and that engaged my attention so much that I went throuth the whole address book. It consists of names of exiles (it was started after our escape from Czechoslovakia) and a few others who live at home and with whom I came in contact during the "thaw." The list of the deceased proved to be more extensive than I would have expected. There are a few dozen names on my list, a substantial part of my address book. But what moved me most was that the names dated from recent times. It clarified to me what a friend said last week: "Did you know that three of our friends died last week?" and he named them. He added that never in his life did it seem to him that people died as often as now. And he was absolutely right. In our generation of older exiles, it is true and cannot be otherwise.

Soon it occurred to me that one day I could also be on such a list—not on my own but that of my friends. It pleases me that up to now they have not had to cross my name out. But it will happen. I do not know how soon, but I know that it is inevitable. Even their lists turn out more and more to be lists of the deceased. They make them unknowingly, just as I do. And I have to say that we all show a certain tenacity. The lists grow longer and richer, and will grow even longer in the future. Only my list and those of my former students who live in exile will last a little longer. They are many years younger than I. In the long run, out of my list of names will remain just a small list of the living, which, however, will not be of use to anyone.

My former list of friends is therefore understandably changing. The names remain basically the same, but the relationship of the living to the dead constantly changes in favor of the dead. Against my will, the list of the living changes into a list of the deceased. I do not want to draw it up; it makes itself, and it cannot be arrested. In the end nobody will use it. Perhaps someday a man interested in the history of our exile will find it and will discover how the addresses of the distinguished addressees have changed. Maybe he will say: "Look at that, Mr. N.W. was first in Munich, then in Paris, then in London, and in the end received a professorship at Cornell. Now I have to find out when he moved and for what reasons and whether he remained at this last address until his death."

The transformation of an address book into a list of the deceased happens everywhere. Our exile is no exception. The deceased are normally replaced by the newly born. In exile it happens more in a biological way than in a human way. How many of the newly born children will speak Czech, and how many will consider themselves Czech? Maybe some, but not many. Thus do the lists of the deceased become lists of a dying branch, sentenced by the Communists to extinction. I do not mean physical extinction (they had no influence on that), which is the fate of all people, but cultural and national extinction as well. This is their unforgivable mistake, their historical crime, whose extent and effects they are unaware of. But even if they were, they would have no pangs of conscience. The guilt complex died out with Lenin. A true-blooded Communist is never guilty. He does not recognize any moral concepts in a political fight whatsoever: Everything is acceptable, if it favors Communism, everything is allowed. I believe that no other politician in the history of the world, even if we think of Machiavelli or Bismarck, left behind such an immoral legacy, incorporated into a bureaucratic apparatus, as did this indirect originator of our list of deceased in exile.

What strikes me most about these lists of the deceased is the inevitability of their existence and the constant irresistibility of their growth and size. Yes, even my list will grow, and it will be written by my own hand. It seems terrible to me, but what can I do? Nothing. I have to continue and reconcile myself to it. But now that I know how many deceased there are in it, I shall use it only carefully and, if possible, seldom.

★   ★   ★

This last story of my husband's was written in the late spring of 1970. Two months later, he was no longer living.

J.M.